HENRY V
A HISTORY OF HIS MOST IMPORTANT PLACES AND EVENTS

HENRY V
A HISTORY OF HIS MOST IMPORTANT PLACES AND EVENTS

DEBORAH FISHER

Pen & Sword
HISTORY
AN IMPRINT OF PEN & SWORD BOOKS LTD.
YORKSHIRE – PHILADELPHIA

First published in Great Britain in 2022 by
PEN AND SWORD HISTORY
An imprint of
Pen & Sword Books Ltd
Yorkshire – Philadelphia

Copyright © Deborah Fisher, 2022

ISBN 978 1 39907 046 1

The right of Deborah Fisher to be identified as Author of this work has been asserted by him in accordance with the Copyright, Designs and Patents Act 1988.

A CIP catalogue record for this book is available from the British Library.

All rights reserved. No part of this book may be reproduced or transmitted in any form or by any means, electronic or mechanical including photocopying, recording or by any information storage and retrieval system, without permission from the Publisher in writing.

Typeset in Times New Roman 12/16 by
SJmagic DESIGN SERVICES, India.
Printed and bound in the UK by CPI Group (UK) Ltd.

Pen & Sword Books Limited incorporates the imprints of Atlas, Archaeology, Aviation, Discovery, Family History, Fiction, History, Maritime, Military, Military Classics, Politics, Select, Transport, True Crime, Air World, Frontline Publishing, Leo Cooper, Remember When, Seaforth Publishing, The Praetorian Press, Wharncliffe Local History, Wharncliffe Transport, Wharncliffe True Crime and White Owl.

For a complete list of Pen & Sword titles please contact
PEN & SWORD BOOKS LIMITED
47 Church Street, Barnsley, South Yorkshire, S70 2AS, England
E-mail: enquiries@pen-and-sword.co.uk
Website: www.pen-and-sword.co.uk

Or

PEN AND SWORD BOOKS
1950 Lawrence Rd, Havertown, PA 19083, USA
E-mail: Uspen-and-sword@casematepublishers.com
Website: www.penandswordbooks.com

Contents

Acknowledgements		vi
Introduction		vii
Chapter 1	Monmouth and Courtfield	1
Chapter 2	Prince of Wales	14
Chapter 3	Shrewsbury	19
Chapter 4	Campaigning in Wales – Aberystwyth and Harlech	30
Chapter 5	Early Kingship – Kenilworth and other Royal Residences	42
Chapter 6	The Road to Agincourt	54
Chapter 7	Second French Campaign – Rouen and Paris	92
Chapter 8	France: The Final Campaign	140
Conclusion		151
Epilogue		160
Appendix	How to Follow in the Footsteps of Henry of Monmouth	162
Select Bibliography		188
Index		191

Acknowledgements

It would not have been possible for me to write this book without the careful research into the period already done by distinguished historians, particularly Anne Curry and Juliet Barker. I can claim no personal credit for their work and I have drawn on it extensively.

I would like to thank:

As ever, Phil Carradice, for help and advice whenever I needed it.

Bob Cowie, the Syon Abbey Society, and my friend Lorraine Mepham, for archaeological input.

The MonmouthpediA project, led by John Cummings. Throughout my research, Wikipedia has been used as it is intended to be used – not as a direct reference, but as a source of citations and useful summaries.

The late Rhys Jones, a reliable and always enthusiastic friend and collaborator.

Introduction

It is 600 years since the death of King Henry V, one of England's best-known kings. Many books have been written about his life, a majority of which concentrate entirely on his victory at the Battle of Agincourt in 1415. Shakespeare, in his cycle of history plays, depicted Henry in a flattering but largely realistic manner, showing the wayward young man as well as the inspirational warrior. The plays were based on history as Shakespeare knew it, but the story they told was some way from the truth. They have misled many people into believing that Agincourt was Henry V's main achievement, and that the circumstances of that achievement were very different from what they actually were.

Shakespeare did not invent everything he wrote from scratch, but he was born over a century after Henry died, and had to rely on earlier writers whose idea of history was very different from our own. Not only did medieval chroniclers tend to be prejudiced in favour of their home countries – thus English and French writers give contradictory versions of Henry's actions – but they were writing 'history' as a story, and did not hesitate to embellish that story with details that they felt would make it more interesting to their readers. Few of them had witnessed at first hand the events about which they wrote. Fortunately, documentary records exist for the period that have enabled modern historians to reconstruct the facts and events of Henry's career in a more impartial and more realistic way. It is the everyday records, ranging from the proceedings of parliament to parish registers, shopping lists and invoices, that enable us to place him in certain places at certain times. Archaeological investigation also continues to play an important role in any attempt to visualise the past.

This book, in keeping with its place in the *Following in the Footsteps* series, is a kind of travelogue, concentrating on places that were important in Henry's life, many of which can still be visited by those interested in getting a better feel for the man and understanding how his character was shaped by his environment. Perhaps it is wrong to suggest that it is literally possible to follow in Henry's footsteps. Records of his reign and activities are plentiful but cannot always give an exact picture of where he was at a given time. The roads he took, particularly during his military campaigns in Wales and France, may no longer be passable; they may have been abandoned or built over, or perhaps were never known to anyone outside Henry's immediate circle. Nevertheless, those who at least make the attempt to pass the same way as Henry will discover that he was far more than a one-battle-wonder.

Henry V was not born to rule. Despite being the great-grandson of a king, he was born in a small country town, far from London, and spent much of his youth on military campaigns in Ireland, Wales and the Marches. After his father usurped the throne in 1400, he helped resist Owain Glyndŵr's rebellion and became battle-hardened as a teenager when he received a near-fatal wound at Shrewsbury in 1403. Despite falling out with his father and at one time being expelled from the government, he quickly reinvented himself as a model king, and set his eyes firmly on the prospect of the crown of France. Thereafter, much of his nine-year reign was spent on military campaigns beyond the British Isles. The Battle of Agincourt, at the height of his powers, was one of the most spectacular victories ever won by an English army, but it is not the whole story.

The book takes its reader on a journey from the rural areas around Monmouth, where Henry was born, to the magnificent royal court of his father's cousin and enemy, King Richard II. It takes us into the wilds of Wales and across the sea to the even wilder Irish landscape, where the teenage boy won his spurs and was knighted by King Richard. We follow his short-lived career as a student at Oxford. We see the prince reunited with his father in England, and we travel with him into battle at Shrewsbury against his father's former supporters. We see him capture Harlech Castle from the rebel followers of a rival 'Prince of Wales'. We witness his coronation at Westminster Abbey, and visit his private retreat at Kenilworth. As king, we see him seize Harfleur and then take the long road towards Calais, culminating in the battle for which he will always be best remembered. Thereafter, we follow his continued campaigning in France as he struggles to get a firm hold on the French crown, his marriage to Catherine of Valois at Troyes, and his eventual, tragically premature, death at the Château de Vincennes.

What emerges is a picture of a man much influenced by his environment, both the physical environment and the company of those he encountered in the course of his travels. All personalities are, at least in part, the product of experience, but this is particularly true of King Henry V. Those who know his story seldom fail to be both fascinated and moved by it, and this makes him an ideal subject for the study that follows.

Chapter 1

Monmouth and Courtfield

Monarchs of the Middle Ages spent more of their time on the road than we tend to realise. Sometimes this was for diplomatic reasons, sometimes for military reasons, and sometimes simply to give their subjects an opportunity to see them, thus inspiring widespread loyalty. King Richard I, 'the Lionheart', famously spent only around six months of his ten-year reign in his kingdom. Often, especially under the Plantagenets, the heir to the throne would pass substantial amounts of time out of the country, cutting his kingly teeth in England's overseas possessions. At the time of his birth, Henry of Monmouth, though directly descended from King Edward III, was never meant to be King of England. Nevertheless, almost from birth, he was a traveller, spending much of his youth in the principality of Wales.

He was born within the lands of his father, Henry Bolingbroke, one of the many cousins of the reigning king, Richard II. Bolingbroke, generally known by the name of his birthplace in Lincolnshire, was born in 1367, the eldest surviving son of the marriage between John of Gaunt, a son of King Edward III, and Blanche of Lancaster, an heiress who brought with her a dukedom and considerable property. Bolingbroke was married off at the age of about fourteen, to another valuable heiress, Mary de Bohun, who was approximately the same age. One version of the story says that Mary had been promised to a convent by her greedy brother-in-law, none other than John of Gaunt's younger brother Thomas, who hoped to inherit the whole of Mary's father's estates, but he was foiled in this attempt to enrich himself when Bolingbroke took her for his wife.

Although we know the birth date of Henry V – 16 September – there has always been some doubt as to the year of his birth, but there is good evidence for it having taken place in 1386. At that time, King Richard II was himself only nineteen and had not yet married the first of his two wives. It was assumed that he would at some point father an heir. After Richard, there were matrilineal descendants of Edward III who could claim the throne for their children, and the heir presumptive was Roger Mortimer, Earl of March. After Mortimer and his sons, however, the best claim was that of Richard's uncle, John of Gaunt, the grandfather of the newly-born Prince Henry.

According to tradition, Henry was born in Monmouth, where his mother had previously been delivered of another son who had not survived. It is a common fallacy that Henry was not born in Wales – some suggest that Monmouthshire was then in England, others that he was in fact born at Courtfield, a manor in the village of Welsh Bicknor, on the other side of the river Severn and thus in England; the theory is that his mother and her attendants were unable to reach Monmouth Castle in time for the birth. Even if this were true, it would not make Henry English-born. The parish of Welsh Bicknor is now in Herefordshire, but in the 1380s it was an 'exclave' of Monmouthshire (hence the name of the village). The sixth-century British saint, Dubricius, known to the Welsh as Dyfrig, was the bishop of the diocese that is now Llandaff, and the land on which the church was established at Welsh Bicknor was specifically granted to him in a charter dated to his lifetime. Not until 1542 did an ambiguity in the wording of Henry VIII's Act of Union lead to a belief that Monmouthshire itself had been moved into England, and even after that, the region of Herefordshire between the rivers Monnow and Wye was largely Welsh-speaking.

The town of Monmouth takes great pride in its most famous son. Outside the Shire Hall stands a garish sculpture, dating from 1792, intended to represent King Henry V; its poor quality and lack of historical verisimilitude has brought it few compliments in the intervening years, but it remains a symbol of the town's historical significance, even though it bears the date '1387', which is almost certainly incorrect. The town's main square is named Agincourt Square in tribute to what is still generally considered the king's greatest achievement. The former Henry V public house has long since been converted to an Italian restaurant, but in any case, the building is eighteenth century in origin and has no connection with Henry.

The castle, where Mary de Bohun is reputed to have given birth to the son and heir of Henry Bolingbroke, is nowadays mostly a ruin, hidden away in a side street, but it would have been impressive when it was built in the eleventh century, one of the first new stone castles constructed by the Norman overlords after their conquest of England. It belonged to the ancient earldom of Hereford, which had been created well before the Normans came and had at one time been in the possession of Harold Godwinson, King of England. This did not mean that the English had been in full control of this part of Wales, and neither were the Normans. They were, however, firmly in control of the town of Monmouth. The castle remains are in the care of Cadw and can be visited free of charge. Great Castle House, a seventeenth-century extension to the castle, now houses a regimental museum of the Royal Monmouthshires.

It was in the confusingly named 'Queen's Chamber' in the castle gatehouse that Henry's birth is said to have taken place – Mary died before her husband took the throne, and thus was never queen, but her husband's grandmother, Queen Philippa, had previously slept there, hence the name. Although Mary's father was the late Earl of Hereford, the castle had come into the possession of her father-in-law, John of Gaunt, through his marriage to Blanche of Lancaster, whose inheritance conveyed on him a title and the accompanying large estates. When Henry of Monmouth became king in 1413, the dukedom of Lancaster was merged in the Crown and still belongs to the British monarch.

A church had existed at Monmouth since the seventh century, but there is little evidence of permanent settlement before the Norman invasion, yet by the time of the Domesday Book in 1085, a town existed. Monnow Street, which runs through the centre of the town, is unmistakably medieval in plan. The burgage plots – individual rented properties on long narrow strips of land whose outlines are traced by present-day houses and gardens – were laid out in the fifty years following the Battle of Hastings. By 1386, the settlement had expanded considerably and the suburb of Overmonnow had been built, even though the town was not yet, technically, a borough. Its prosperity was partly based on a thriving local iron industry, which made use of charcoal from the nearby Forest of Dean.

The build-up of defences over the next few centuries reveals that the townspeople were in regular fear of attack, either from Wales or from their warring English countrymen. The town walls were built around 1300, and the bridge over the Monnow, said to be the only fortified river bridge in Britain, was constructed at about the same time. One puzzle for architectural historians is why the unique Monnow Gate, which originally had a portcullis, is located in the middle of the bridge rather than at one end. This is not really explained by the fact that it probably doubled as a toll gate, controlling public access to local markets. There are records of additional tariffs being charged on goods brought by this route, including such items as pigs, honey and roofing nails. The bridge is now pedestrianised, and the upper rooms over the gate, which once housed a small museum, are accessible to visitors only by means of a guided tour.

In 2012, Wikipedia volunteers launched the 'Monmouthpedia' collaborative project, as a result of which visitors to the town were able, for the first time, to read QR codes with their smartphones, leading them directly to Wikipedia articles about each specific feature they were looking at. The codes are distributed around the town, and the articles available include over fifty buildings and structures, as well as numerous historical events and people relevant to the town. Monmouth thus earned the title of 'the world's first Wikipedia town'.

The Wikipedia project followed on from the establishment of a 'Monmouth Heritage Trail' in 2009, with the object of assisting visitors in finding the most interesting of the town's historic buildings. These include the White Swan Inn, whose name goes back at least as far as the eighteenth century and could conceivably be a reference to Mary de Bohun (on account of the family emblem being a swan collared and chained); the present building is much later in date. The Robin Hood Inn, which dates from the fifteenth century, may have been in existence in Henry's lifetime, and its frontage, with a four-centre doorway at ground level, gives some idea of what many inns must have looked like in those days. The Queen's Head probably dates from the following century.

Another public house, the Old Nag's Head, though much later in date, incorporates a section of the medieval town wall, in the form of a drum-shaped tower. This tower is the only surviving piece of the town's fortifications, and was part of the 'Dixton Gate', the rest of which was demolished in 1770. The remains of the tower are best viewed from the outside of the building. Intriguingly, there was a Congregationalist meeting house adjacent to the Dixton Gate until the early nineteenth century, when the congregation moved to a new building in Glendower Street, now known as Glendower House. Despite the name, there is no historical connection between either the street or the former chapel and Henry's contemporary, Owain Glyndŵr, after whom both were named.

The medieval monastic buildings attached to the former Benedictine priory would certainly have been present in Henry's time, though they have been substantially rebuilt and altered. The priory, dating from the late eleventh century, was dissolved in 1536, but was thriving a hundred years earlier. However, the only surviving medieval feature is a remarkable fifteenth-century window, sometimes called 'Geoffrey's window' in honour of Geoffrey of Monmouth (died c.1155), who may have been associated with the priory but could never have seen the window in question. The present St Mary's Church, with its 200-foot spire towering over the town, largely dates from the eighteenth and nineteenth centuries, but does incorporate parts of the original priory church.

That Geoffrey of Monmouth was associated with the town in some way is beyond doubt, since he referred to himself as 'Galfridus Monemutensis'. His writings are evidence of his familiarity with the area, and he may well have been born there, but this does not mean that he was Welsh; he probably had Norman blood. Although Geoffrey remains best known for his *Historia Regum Britanniae* (History of the Kings of Britain), a fanciful and popular account of the history of Britain from its ancient beginnings, he was in fact a priest who rose to the position of Bishop of St Asaph towards the end of his life. Despite having spent most of his career in Norman England, he was one of the prime instigators of the legend of King Arthur, which appears to be heavily influenced by Celtic myth. His 'History' was widely translated and is likely to have been on the reading list of the young Lord Henry. It would not be surprising if it inspired him to see himself as England's new Arthur.

The 'Monmouth cap', the traditional headgear of local men (including soldiers of Henry V's army), was a knitted garment of local wool, produced by a regional cottage industry, whose practicality quickly made it popular throughout England and Wales. The only surviving example of a sixteenth-century Monmouth cap can be viewed at Monmouth's town museum. That this item of clothing was known to originate from Wales is backed up by Shakespeare, admittedly writing nearly 200 years later. The dramatist, in his play of the same name, has Henry V, when he is in disguise and being questioned by Pistol the night before the Battle of Agincourt, say, 'I am a Welshman' (referencing both his birthplace and his ancestry). He later repeats the claim to Fluellen, saying, 'For I am Welsh, you know'.

One of the reasons for Shakespeare's insistence on Henry's nationality is that in 1598, when he was writing the play, the current monarch was Queen Elizabeth, granddaughter of King Henry VII, who was himself a quarter Welsh by descent and also born in Wales. Elizabeth had many Welsh courtiers and servants and it is claimed that she herself sometimes wore a leek on St David's Day in recognition of her ancestry. So it is not surprising that Fluellen tells the king:

> Your majesty says very true: if your majestie is remembered of it, the Welshmen did good service in a garden where leeks did grow, wearing leeks in their Monmouth caps; which, your majesty knows, to this hour is an honourable badge of the service; and I do believe your majesty takes no scorn to wear the leek upon Saint Davy's day.

Towards the middle of her reign, Elizabeth's parliament would even introduce legislation to compel men of a certain rank to wear English or Welsh-made woollen caps, in an attempt to protect native industries and reduce imports of more fashionable foreign-made headgear. Her nobles supported the attempt; even the Earl of Shrewsbury is known to have possessed such a cap.

As will be seen in later chapters, although Bolingbroke enjoyed hunting in the nearby Forest of Dean, he and his family did not spend much of their lives at Monmouth. His lands were extensive and they moved from one property to another as suited them. The town did, however, escape any damage during the rebellion of Owain Glyndŵr, by which time Bolingbroke was King of England.

*****

Like her mother-in-law, Blanche of Lancaster, Henry's mother, Mary de Bohun, died in her twenties, shortly after giving birth to her youngest child. Her eldest son was about eight by this time, and remarkably, all six children survived into adulthood. Henry's younger siblings were born at various locations, depending on the family's circumstances at the time: Thomas in London, Blanche and Philippa in Peterborough, John and Humphrey at places unknown. Despite this, Henry and his younger brothers would remain close, and loyal to one another, throughout their lives. Despite having died at Peterborough, Mary was buried in Leicester, at the Church of the Annunciation of Our Lady of the Newarke, a church that no longer exists – though some of its original stonework is displayed at the heritage centre of De Montfort University.

Whether or not he was born there, 'The Lord Henry' really was at the manor of Courtfield, in Welsh Bicknor, during much of this period, possibly from a very early age, coming under the care of Lady Margaret Montagu (died 1395) and subsequently of her daughter-in-law, the Countess of Salisbury, whose eldest son Thomas was almost of an age with Henry. His first nursemaid appears to have been a woman called Johanna Waring, to whom he would one day grant an annual pension of £20.

An oak cradle and a bed purportedly used by Henry at Courtfield were still being shown off to visitors for centuries afterwards. The owners of Troy House, built at Mitchel Troy (three miles from Monmouth) in the seventeenth century for the Herbert family, at one time claimed to possess not only the cradle and bed belonging to Henry V but also a suit of armour supposedly worn by him as a boy for training purposes. Even nineteenth-century visitors like the Reverend Thomas Dudley Fosbroke recognised this as being of completely the wrong date. The oaken cradle, or one like it, was a less obvious fake. When auctioned in 1908, it was purchased by none other than King Edward VII, who had so long been associated with the title of Prince of Wales that he must have found it difficult to get out of the habit. He donated it to the London Museum in 1912, and it can still be seen there, but it is now known to be of a much later date.

St Margaret's Church, completely rebuilt in the 1850s, is near Courtfield manor and now belongs to the Vaughan estate. Its most interesting feature, in terms of the life of Henry V, is an effigy of a lady from the medieval period, transferred from the old Norman church. This is believed to represent either Lady Margaret Montagu or her daughter-in-law, Countess Maud. Lady Margaret's tomb is, however, to be found in the church at Goodrich, an older building within the same parish. The Salisbury family were staunch supporters of King Richard II, and the earl would lose his life as a result of his opposition to Bolingbroke's coup.

The medieval manor of Courtfield stood in a loop of the River Wye, offering some natural defences, and was probably fortified. The private house that now stands on the site is not the one that Henry knew, but a nineteenth-century construction, built over the original foundations. Courtfield is said to have been particularly difficult to access, and some have cited this as a reason for Bolingbroke's children being sent there. Their father spent the whole of 1390 campaigning in Lithuania, whither he returned on a second campaign two years later, then went on pilgrimage to Jerusalem. The church lives up to this reputation for remoteness, and past members of the congregation were in the habit of arriving by boat. Even now, with a car, reaching it requires some effort.

At Courtfield, Henry must have received a basic education. He quickly learned to speak and write English, French and Latin, and he later acquired a substantial personal library, at a time when the printing press was yet to be developed. His love of literature is something he may have inherited from his father, who, despite his frequent military ventures and pursuit of activities, was a highly cultured man, fond of books and music. In addition to his textbooks, one volume the Lord Henry definitely possessed was an edition of Geoffrey Chaucer's poem *Troilus and Criseyde* that still survives. Chaucer, who died in 1400, was not only popular with the general reader but was closely associated with the royal family by the happy accident of his wife's sister, Katherine Swynford, having become the mistress, and later wife, of Henry's grandfather, John of Gaunt.

A year after Mary de Bohun's death, Henry of Monmouth was to be found at Leicester, where it is recorded that he received a visit from a doctor. As a child, he is reputed by some to have been a weakling, but other purchases of equipment for him that are mentioned in the records also suggest that by the time he left Courtfield he was beginning to practise outdoor pursuits, as well as developing an interest in music. He learned to play several instruments and there is evidence that in adulthood he composed some settings of parts of the Mass which are credited to 'Roy Henry'. A band of musicians followed him everywhere he held court.

Hunting was a pastime considered suitable for noble youths, partly because of its perceived similarity to war. Although skills in archery were somewhat looked down on, this being the pastime of commoners, Henry would have learned to use a longbow and crossbow as well as a sword and spear. Indeed, he demonstrated these skills later in life. Hunting was also a way of improving horsemanship, in which warriors of rank needed to be expert. However, more advanced training was required before he would achieve such a status. For this, the family would initially look to his grandfather.

*****

With a father who was seldom at home and spent long periods overseas, the young Henry of Monmouth became quite attached to his uncle, King Richard II. Their relationship remained close even after Richard, in a clumsy attempt to avoid a diplomatic incident, exiled Bolingbroke from England in 1398 (with the approval of John of Gaunt). Thereafter, the king continued to treat Henry in accordance with his place in the line of succession, making him an annual allowance of £500.

As time went on and Richard's first wife failed to produce any children, Henry's status as a contingency heir had begun to be recognised. Richard's second wife was a child when they married in 1396, and would not be capable of conceiving for at least another five or six years. Richard made financial provision for Henry, and he was soon being considered as a potential husband for Marie, the daughter of John, Duke of Brittany. Nothing came of this plan, nor of the alternative plan to marry off the youthful Marie to Henry's widowed father! A few years later, after the death of the Duke of Brittany, Henry Bolingbroke would marry Marie's mother, Joan of Navarre.

In 1398, shortly before his father's exile, Henry seems to have passed out of his grandfather's supervision to become a student at the Queen's College, Oxford, where his uncle, Henry Beaufort, Bishop of Lincoln, was Chancellor of the University. The college has been extensively rebuilt in the centuries since, but there is a tradition that Henry's lodgings were above the college gate, in the section of the former building that stood opposite St Edmund Hall, overlooking what is now called Queen's Lane. He was not there for more than a few months, and there is no record of his studies, but he remained close to Beaufort throughout his life.

The period as Richard's protégé marked the beginning of Henry's real military training, and he was quickly removed from Oxford. A medieval illustration shows the young Henry being knighted by the king, during his subsequent campaign in Ireland. Henry was no more than thirteen years old at the time. This was Richard's second Irish expedition, and it had become necessary after the failure of an attempt by his heir presumptive, Roger Mortimer, to bring the English possessions in Ireland back into order; in the course of the attempt, Mortimer was killed in battle, and his son Edmund inherited his place in the order of succession. The following summer, Richard set out to make his authority over Ireland felt.

Richard's second Irish expedition went less well than a previous campaign five years earlier, which meant that young Henry learned about the hardships of military service at first hand. The large force set sail from Milford Haven in south Wales in April 1399, two months after the death of John of Gaunt, and Henry was not the only youth present in the party; the teenage sons of a number of nobles accompanied Richard. There seems to have been some unease in England (perhaps with hindsight) at the manner in which Richard departed, taking his crown jewels with him, and telling his second wife, nine-year-old Isabelle of Valois, that she would soon be joining him there.

At the outset, Richard seems to have had no ulterior motive for taking Henry to Ireland. However, when he heard that Bolingbroke had invaded England in his absence, he confined both Henry of Monmouth and Henry's cousin Humphrey at Trim Castle (a Mortimer possession), effectively holding them hostage. Trim was the largest castle the Normans built in Ireland. Its Norman keep and most of the defensive curtain wall survive today and can be visited. By the 1390s it was two hundred years old and would have been a very forbidding place, well suited to intimidating prisoners. Humphrey (the son of Henry's late uncle, Thomas of Woodstock) died in Anglesey on the return journey, and it is not certain how long Henry himself remained a hostage. He is known to have been back in England by October 1399, when he took a ceremonial role at his father's coronation at Westminster Abbey, and he was invested as Prince of Wales two days later.

Henry of Monmouth was knighted (again) and received the Order of the Garter the day before the coronation, in an age-old ceremony that began with ritual bathing – to remove one's sins – before being dressed in a white robe and red cloak and spending the night in a vigil of prayer. Having achieved this, the candidate was presented with a sword and spurs, and was dubbed by the king. Thirteen was not at all an unusual age for this to occur, and several other youths, including Henry's younger brothers, were knighted at the same time.

It may have been difficult for Henry to reconcile his previous affection for King Richard with his father's actions and the personal advantages brought him by the latter. Bolingbroke had known that Richard would land in Wales on his return from Ireland, and the king was soon deserted by many of his followers. Forced to divide up his fleet, he was in an impossibly weak position by the time Bolingbroke sent Henry Percy, Earl of Northumberland, to Conway Castle to negotiate a surrender. The king was lured to Flint Castle on a promise of his life being spared if he would abdicate. He was taken to London, where he was placed in the Tower. However, Richard was not without his adherents, particularly when Bolingbroke, who was not next in line, decided to take the throne for himself instead of merely claiming his late father's dukedom as he had promised when he arrived in England. The 'Epiphany Rising" resulted in several executions (including that of Henry of Monmouth's former guardian, the Earl of Salisbury), and Richard was moved to Pontefract Castle, where he was starved to death.

Chapter 2

Prince of Wales

It was by no means a foregone conclusion that the heir to the throne would be given the title of Prince of Wales, a title that had been vacant since Richard II acceded to the throne in 1377. Henry of Monmouth's investiture was Bolingbroke's way of emphasising not only the fact that he had established himself as king, but that the succession was assured. It was also the start of the Lancastrian dynasty, leading slowly but inexorably to the Wars of the Roses. The prince's household quickly grew, along with his possessions. Many of those who were appointed to serve him as Prince of Wales would go on to be lifelong supporters. Some, such as Sir Robert Corbet, would be involved in the Agincourt campaign. John Waterton, who had been a servant of John of Gaunt, would serve Henry IV and Henry V and become one of the country's leading diplomats.

It is assumed that, after leaving Courtfield, Henry of Monmouth had gone into service as a page in the household of his grandfather, John of Gaunt, at Leicester Castle. That castle was part of the legacy that Richard II had tried to take from Bolingbroke; it would become an official royal residence when Henry IV became king and would continue to be one until the middle of the fifteenth century. The name of Peter Melbourne, an official of the duchy of Lancaster, occurs frequently in the records, and this man may have acted as a kind of guardian to Henry after the death of John of Gaunt early in 1399. He was clearly an influential figure in Henry's life, and was appointed the Prince of Wales's chamberlain by 1401.

Leicester Castle, a Norman construction on the banks of the River Soar, has mostly disappeared, but parts of the walls survive.

The remains of the original motte can be seen in Castle Yard, and the original great hall, which would have been very familiar to the young Lord Henry, formed the basis of the present building, despite its outwardly modern appearance. John of Gaunt is believed to have died in this room, a spot where Henry V, as king, would hold court twenty years later, while his parliament discussed measures to control the Lollards. Records of the building in Gaunt's time mention a parlour, a kitchen and larder, a dungeon and a 'great chamber'. The gun loops visitors will notice in the section of the original castle wall, next to the 'Turret Gateway', were added much later, during the English Civil War, when the city was attacked by Royalist forces.

'Castle House', as it is now known, gradually fell into disrepair in the sixteenth century, and was converted during the reign of Queen Anne. Thereafter it was used as an assembly room as well as a courthouse. These days it is operated by Leicester City Council, and guided tours are available. The external appearance of the building is deceptive, since the earthworks survive within the castle grounds, and the courtyard known as the 'Newarke' (the 'new work'), dating from the fourteenth century, contains the Turret Gateway and the Magazine Gateway. De Montfort University, whose campus is located near the castle, opened a new heritage centre in 2015. The Hawthorne Building, which houses the exhibition, was built in the 1890s, and stands within the Newarke, incorporating some of the ruins of the Church of Our Lady. This is where Mary de Bohun, Henry's mother was buried, so it would certainly have become very familiar to him. Her remains were later re-interred in the chapel of Trinity Hospital, which had been built by Henry of Grosmont (1310-1361), John of Gaunt's father-in-law.

There appears to be some confusion as to whether the chapel in question is now the church of St Mary de Castro ('St Mary of the Castle'), which may stand on its foundations. The demolition of the spire of St Mary's in 2014, for structural reasons, leaves a square tower, the base of which can be clearly viewed from inside the church, because of its idiosyncratic method of construction. If Mary was indeed reburied there, her tomb can no longer be seen, but her remains are thought to have been buried close to the high altar.

The prince's mother had been descended through her mother, Joan Fitzalan, from an earlier Roger Mortimer, himself the grandson of Llywelyn the Great through Llywelyn's daughter Gwladus Ddu. Thus King Henry V and his siblings were all directly descended from the princes of Gwynedd, which is more than can be said for his father's Welsh rival, Owain Glyndŵr. Henry's claim to be a true prince of Wales is often overlooked for the simplest of reasons. Although the Welsh, prior to their country being annexed by England, had laws that were in many ways progressive and liberal, it was simply not possible for a woman to inherit a kingdom. Because Henry's Welsh ancestry came through the female line, it has been largely ignored. Henry V is also believed to be the first King of England since the conquest who did not speak French on a day-to-day basis, although it remained an official language, and this was something the average Englishman welcomed.

Ironically, as soon as Bolingbroke achieved the throne of England, he sought to marry off his eldest son to the eldest daughter of King Charles VI of France. The lady in question, Isabelle of Valois, was in fact the widow of Henry's uncle, King Richard II, but she was closer in age to Henry, and his father had no wish to return her dowry. Although their paths must have crossed during the short period when she was nominally Queen of England, she and the prince may not have known one another well, simply because she had not spent a great deal of time in her husband's company. For whatever reason, the marriage negotiations failed. Isabelle returned to France, and was married off to a more suitable French nobleman, Charles d'Orléans (who would reappear later in Henry's life). Another scheme for Henry's marriage was devised later, in 1402, when negotiations were beginning for the marriage of Henry's youngest sister Philippa to King Eric of Norway; the idea was mooted of a marriage between Henry and King Eric's sister Catherine, but although Philippa's wedding took place, no union with Catherine of Pomerania occurred.

Immediately after his father's accession, the king decided it was time for his eldest son to continue his training in the art of war, and together they led a substantial English army to make war on Scotland. The campaign is generally considered to have been a disaster; in the fortnight Henry IV spent in the country, he found the Scots to be intransigent, and his troops did 'little damage'. Among the new king's most important supporters were Henry Percy, Earl of Northumberland, and his son, also Henry Percy but known to history as 'Harry Hotspur'. Both had encouraged him to take the throne. The Prince of Wales knew the family well: Northumberland's brother, the Earl of Worcester, would be appointed his governor in 1401, and Worcester's nephew, Hotspur, became something of a mentor to him. Henry IV, however, was already growing uneasy about the amount of power wielded by the Percys in the northern parts of his kingdom.

The aim of the northern campaign was to bring King Robert III of Scotland to heel, and the English king sought to revive his ancestral claim to the Scottish throne. The earls of the Scottish border lands had been taking advantage of the disruption caused by Bolingbroke's invasion to plunder the north of England, and he had retaliated by offering asylum to some of the Scottish king's enemies. The Scots, knowing that Henry IV was short of money, declined to face him in open battle. There was little gained from the invasion, and a truce was soon called. It would be left to the Percys to quell the Scots.

One of the biggest threats to Henry IV's reign was the Welsh rebellion under Owain Glyndŵr, which broke out in September 1400, while the king was busy in Scotland. Owain's grievances against neighbouring English landowners had been ignored by the king, so, instead of responding to a call for him to provide fighting men to follow the royal party to Scotland, he used them to launch his own campaign. Despite his tender age, Prince Henry was expected to take a lead in subduing Wales, and a campaign headquarters was set up in Chester on his behalf; he was of course Earl of Chester as well as Prince of Wales.

Chester Castle was an eleventh-century edifice, constructed on the orders of Hugh d'Avranches, the second of its Norman earls. Its original mound survives, but the castle has been subject to considerable rebuilding and modernisation over the centuries. Today it houses a museum and law courts. The 'Agricola Tower' is one of the places where King Richard II had been held prisoner just a few months before Henry's arrival, and the chapel, which the prince would surely have used regularly, dates from around 1300.

It was not, however, until May 1401 that Henry of Monmouth was personally drawn into the hostilities. Owain had taken Conway Castle, and Harry Hotspur, with the prince's assistance, was expected to win it back for the king. The castle fell under the control of two of Owain's relations, Rhys and Gwilym ap Tudur, who negotiated a surrender with Percy that entailed a royal pardon for both of them. The siege took too long for the king's liking, and he countermanded Percy and decided to lead the next attack on Wales in person, though a settlement was eventually negotiated in June to enable Conway to be given up. With the Welsh adopting guerrilla tactics, the king's campaign failed to progress, and Hotspur, put out by the lack of appreciation of his expertise, returned to the north of England to concentrate on his own affairs. Owain Glyndŵr now began to concentrate his efforts on the southern counties of Wales. This time the king was defeated by the weather.

Chapter 3

Shrewsbury

The young prince, now operating from Shrewsbury, was hampered by a lack of funds, complaining to his father that he had been forced to sell his own jewels in order to pay his troops. By this time, King Henry owed the Percy family an estimated £20,000, and they were not willing to wait any longer. The king had mismanaged his response to the rebellion to the extent that they were prepared to ally themselves with its leader, Owain Glyndŵr. Owain had no designs on the English crown. He worked with the Percys on the ostensible basis that Henry IV was not the rightful king, encouraging popular rumours that Richard II was still alive and could be returned to the throne if Henry was defeated. As the son of the Black Prince, King Richard II had acquired a strong following in his father's principality, and they were ready to embrace the idea that they could right great wrongs by putting a dent in the English war machine.

Shrewsbury was the gateway to Wales. The Severn surrounded it on three sides, and the Norman bridge over the river, with its five arches and wooden causeway, became known as the 'English Bridge', and was protected by a gatehouse with a drawbridge, enabling road traffic between the two countries to be cut off if necessary. The original bridge was replaced in the eighteenth century. The smaller bridge, known as the 'Welsh Bridge', that also crosses the Severn, was not built until the 1790s. Thus it was possible for the authorities to restrict, if not prevent, trade between Shrewsbury and Wales, and they duly did so during the rebellion, causing almost as much inconvenience to the English market town as to its Welsh suppliers, whose most lucrative product was woollen cloth. The Old Market Hall in the town centre (now an arts venue) is an Elizabethan building, but there is known to have been a market hall on the same site since the mid-twelfth century.

Shrewsbury Castle, at the time the prince had his headquarters there, bore little resemblance to the present structure. Built shortly after the Norman invasion, by the Marcher lord Roger de Montgomery, the first Earl of Shrewsbury, it had been constructed for the express purpose of intimidating the local population and acting as a base for Roger to launch attacks on the Welsh, and on anyone else who challenged his authority. It was not, however, rebuilt in stone until the twelfth century. By the time Henry of Monmouth took up residence there, it had not seen any serious fighting for about a hundred years. In the sixteenth century, it would pass into humbler ownership, and successive refurbishments altered its appearance greatly, until in the twentieth century it was turned into council offices. Nowadays it houses the Shropshire Regimental Museum.

Wingfield's Tower, also known as the Town Walls Tower, is the only substantial survivor of the medieval town walls. Originally built during the Welsh wars of the early thirteenth century, the tower was remodelled and made bigger during the reign of Henry IV. When most of the town wall was demolished, the tower was being used as a private residence and workshop. Its owners gave it into the care of the National Trust in 1930, and it is run as part of the Attingham Park estate. The interior is occasionally open to the public.

There is no shortage of original medieval buildings in Shrewsbury. Like Monmouth, the town retains the shape of its medieval plan, but it is considerably larger. The King's Head public house is one of many timber-framed buildings that survive, difficult to date but mostly built slightly later than Henry's time. The Golden Cross, reputedly the town's oldest tavern, probably dates from around 1400, when it was converted from its original role as the sacristy of Old St Chad's Church; the present St Chad's is on a different site. In addition to the famous abbey church, three other surviving church buildings, St Alkmund, St Giles and St Julian, were already standing well before

Henry took up residence in Shrewsbury, though they have all been substantially rebuilt and altered in the intervening centuries.

Tucked away in a side street is the Church of St Mary the Virgin, now redundant as a place of worship. Its construction began in the twelfth century, with the tower and Trinity Chapel added later; the latter was connected with the Drapers Company. The spire is a replacement for an earlier structure which at one point collapsed and fell into the nave. The magnificent 'Jesse Window' was not installed here until the eighteenth century, but Henry may have seen it at its original location, thought to have been St Chad's. Much of the stained glass now to be seen at St Mary's was in fact intended for other churches.

The abbey, located on the other side of the Severn, near the 'English Bridge', was founded in 1083 by the Benedictine order of monks, and the west end had been substantially rebuilt in the thirty or so years prior to Henry of Monmouth's residence in the town, so the abbey church he saw would have been a very impressive building indeed, intended to be worthy of holding the remains of St Winifred, which had been brought there from Wales in the twelfth century. The chronicler Adam of Usk later claimed that Henry, after he became king, went on a pilgrimage from Shrewsbury to the site of Winifred's holy well in Flintshire to pay his respects to the saint. The claim that he went barefoot seems to be unsubstantiated, even if it was the somewhat closer well of the same name in Shropshire that he visited; that he went *on* foot is more believable.

A series of novels by the local author Edith Pargeter (1913-1995), also known as Ellis Peters, focuses on the abbey in the Middle Ages, the central character being Brother Cadfael, a monk with detective skills. The town capitalised on the popularity of the Cadfael books by opening a tourist attraction, the 'Shrewsbury Quest', in 1994. It lasted only until 2001, by which time the television adaptation, with Derek Jacobi in the title role, had ended, Pargeter herself had died, and interest had waned. Located near the abbey, the Shrewsbury

Quest attempted to recreate the abbey as it might have been in the twelfth century, with a scriptorium, cellarium, guest hall and gardens. Although the mythical Cadfael lived nearly 300 years before Henry of Monmouth's time, the life of a Benedictine brother would have changed comparatively little in the interim, thus a good opportunity to imbibe the atmosphere of medieval Shrewsbury has been lost. The Cadfael series of books remains, giving the imaginative reader something to relate to when walking through the present-day town; the author was an expert on the town's history, and is unsurpassed at conveying local colour and atmosphere. In 1997, Pargeter's legacy was assured by the installation of a new stained-glass window by Jane Gray, depicting St Benedict, in Shrewsbury Abbey. The window was paid for by Cadfael enthusiasts.

In 1539, under King Henry VIII, the monastery would be dissolved, not entirely undeservedly since the money Henry of Monmouth had donated for the purpose of a chantry chapel had been misappropriated by then. The abbey church would be lucky to escape the destruction common in this period; it survived only because it continued in use as a parish church. The eastern section is gone, leaving the church a rectangular shape and the nave separated from the tower. Work done in the 1860s by the Gothic Revival architect John Loughborough Pearson resulted in the addition of a mock-Norman clerestory and transepts. More recently, a £300,000 repair project, funded mainly by the National Lottery, was carried out in 2018, leaving the building looking much more presentable than it had been for many decades.

Burials at the abbey included that of William Fitzalan, Lord of Oswestry (1105-1160), an ancestor of Henry on his mother's side. Fitzalan's tomb can no longer be identified, but that of Roger de Montgomery, Shrewsbury's first earl and the builder of the castle as well as founder of the abbey, survives within the abbey church.

*****

Harry Hotspur, who had gained his nickname from his reputation as a fighter, had become frustrated with fighting the Welsh, whose grievances were such as to arouse some sympathy on the other side of the border, and had gone home to Northumberland. His wife Elizabeth was the sister of Edmund Mortimer, a member of a powerful Marcher dynasty and now a captive of the Welsh. Henry IV had failed to ransom the young man in a timely manner, possibly because the Mortimers were direct descendants of Edward III, with a better claim to the throne than his own. The king was pleading poverty as a reason for not paying the troops, just as he had in Scotland, but, at the same time, he refused to consider making terms with the rebels. The result was that Hotspur moved quickly down from the north, and turned up at Shrewsbury in July 1403 to face the king's army in battle, along with his uncle, Thomas Percy, Earl of Worcester.

Cheshire, where Hotspur raised many of his troops, was one of few regions that had held out for Richard II when Henry IV took the throne, and Hotspur's father had obtained important offices both there and in North Wales. The recruits were kitted out with Richard's emblem, a white hart, and were told that Richard himself would be present at a rally in Cheshire in July and they would be able to see for themselves that he was still alive. Needless to say, he did not turn up. Meanwhile, the Percys not only claimed that the army they were raising was for their own protection, but are thought to have sent Henry IV a document charging him with having been responsible for Richard's death.

Things did not go according to plan for Harry Hotspur. He had not anticipated a pitched battle so soon. On arrival at Shrewsbury, he attempted to besiege the town. If he could take possession of it quickly, he would command considerable resources and might have reached an accommodation with the young Prince of Wales or taken him prisoner: either alternative would have given the rebel leader the upper hand in any negotiations with the king. The townspeople's response was to burn down some of the buildings closest to the town's defensive walls, apparently in order to make it more difficult for attackers to scale them. Moreover, the English rebels had expected support from Owain Glyndŵr, who was unaware of any need for urgency. An increasingly anxious Hotspur found himself on the wrong side of the River Severn, and rested in a village called Berwick before encamping near the Augustinian abbey of Haughmond, an establishment closely connected with Henry's Fitzalan ancestors. The abbey's ruins are in the care of English Heritage and are open to the public.

If it came to battle, Hotspur had expected to be faced by a small force, led by the inexperienced Prince of Wales, not realising that the king was within easy reach of the battleground and had received warning of his approach. Had it been Henry of Monmouth he faced, a compromise might have been possible. Hotspur may even have been considering trying to 'turn' the prince, but the king was a different matter. Even after reaching Shrewsbury, the rebel leader was still not expecting the arrival of the royal army. Too late, he found himself outnumbered. The king began to advance on the rebel force the following day and Hotspur sought an advantageous spot to make his stand, taking up position near the village of Harlescott, now an industrial suburb of Shrewsbury. A modern pub/restaurant in the village is named the *Harry Hotspur* in his honour, but has no connection with the man himself.

The Battle of Shrewsbury was the first on English soil where the power of the longbow made itself felt. Some accounts say that the archers on Hotspur's side got the better of the royal army, to the extent that 4,000 men are said to have taken fright and deserted the king. Hotspur had the advantage of the high ground, which increased the effort required from the king's attacking army. One of the outstanding leaders on the royalist side was the youthful Earl of Warwick, Richard Beauchamp, a close friend and mentor of the prince, knighted at the same ceremony, who would continue to support him throughout his military career. For his service in the battle, Warwick was made a Knight of the Garter.

In the course of one of the bloodiest battles of the era, Hotspur was fatally wounded, and the opposition to Henry IV quickly melted away. According to Adam of Usk, at least two other knights had been dressed in armour identical to the king's, in order to act as decoys; if this is true, the ruse worked. After one of the doppelgangers was killed, shouts of 'The King is dead' from Hotspur's hopeful supporters, with the intention of intimidating the enemy, were met with the response 'Hotspur is dead' – which turned out to be true. At this point, the rebel army lost heart. The Earl of Worcester did not have the charisma to carry the day, and he was executed two days after the battle. Others killed in the battle included the twenty-six-year-old Earl of Stafford, fighting on the king's side, and the king's standard-bearer, Sir Walter Blount, who was in his mid-fifties. It is generally thought that the number of casualties on the king's side may have been greater than that on the losing side. Perhaps the result would have been different, had not Hotspur fallen in the battle. There was so much at stake.

Also in the thick of the fighting, on the king's side, was the sixteen-year-old Henry of Monmouth, who by now had a certain amount of military experience and had spent part of the spring capturing and destroying Owain Glyndŵr's homes at Sycharth and Glyndyfrdwy. Henry was in charge of the rearguard and almost lost his life in the battle, for exactly the same reason as Hotspur had – he raised his visor, either for a better view or because he felt too hot. Ironically, or perhaps predictably, his wound was caused by the actions of the archers on the opposing side, many of whom were Welsh, recruited by Hotspur as he progressed through the Marches.

An arrow penetrated the prince's cheek, quite close to his eye; the surgeon later recorded in his notes that it was next to his nose on the left-hand side, and the head was embedded to a depth of six inches. The shaft of the arrow could be broken off, but removing the arrowhead was more of a problem. Anyone who has seen an arrow of that period will understand the effect they might have had on a human body. The prince insisted on continuing to fight, which of course increased the danger of fatal injury even further. Afterwards, he was transported to Kenilworth Castle for treatment. If Henry had not been the heir to the throne, he might well have been written off. King David of Scotland had suffered a similar injury about sixty years earlier and in his case, the tip of the arrow had had to be left in place because it was too dangerous to try to extract it; David had suffered terrible pain for the next twenty years.

Having been removed from the scene of the battle, the prince was not around to see his former governor, the Earl of Worcester, beheaded at Shrewsbury. Nor did he see the body of his former friend Harry Hotspur dug up from its initial resting place in Whitchurch, twenty miles from Shrewsbury, mutilated and paraded successively through Shrewsbury, Chester, London, Bristol and Newcastle upon Tyne. At his tender age, we may wonder how he would have reacted to his father's brutal vengeance, but later in life he would himself prove perfectly capable of similarly ruthless conduct. Hotspur's father, who had not been present at the battle, was spared, but unsurprisingly was removed from his official position as Constable of England. It would be only two years before the earl rebelled again.

*****

Visitors to Shrewsbury will not find many traces of the battle on the ground, since the area where it took place is mostly private agricultural land, and the remains of the battleground were partly obliterated by the construction of the A5124 Shrewsbury by-pass. Nevertheless, a 'heritage park' has been created, with some information panels, describing the progress of the battle and pointing out significant features; a small exhibition centre and shop has been added in recent years, and this visitor centre has now been given the catchy title 'Battlefield 1403'. Public footpaths make up a circular route around the area.

Although, as with so many battlefields, the exact location of the fighting has been challenged by some historians, it remains generally accepted that the site currently identified is indeed where most of the action took place. Archaeological finds have been few and disappointing, but this does not disprove the identification of its location. As with any encounter that involves the movement of horses, a large area may have been covered in the course of the battle, perhaps more than the 100-hectare area of the designated battlefield would indicate.

Much of the action took place in a field of peas, within the manor of Harlescott, a position Hotspur had apparently chosen in the hope that the presence of the crops and some small ponds would cause inconvenience to the king's army. This was about a mile south-west of where the Church of St Mary Magdalene now stands, on the site of a mass grave containing the corpses of some of those killed in the battle. It is often called Battlefield Church, not so much as a legacy of the battle as because the whole village is now known as Battlefield. The church is reputed to have been built in about 1410, traditionally on the specific orders of King Henry IV. If this was the case, it may have had something to do with the regrets he and his son both felt at the death of Hotspur, who had at one time been a friend and ally. The College of St Mary Magdalen was founded simultaneously at Battlefield, under the leadership of Roger Yve, the local rector, who was its first 'master'. Later it would include a school, but it was brought to an end in 1548 along with all other collegiate chantries, and its property was sold off.

*****

Kenilworth Castle, where the wounded Henry of Monmouth was taken to be treated, was a former home of his grandfather, John of Gaunt. It was lucky for him that the royal physician was available – a man named John Bradmore. Bradmore was faced with the difficulty of how to extract the arrowhead from the prince's cheek without killing the patient, and he had to think about the problem for a day or two before he came up with the answer. In the meantime, tutting over the feeble efforts of those who had already given the prince some basic first aid, he treated the wound with honey, and tried to enlarge the hole so that the arrow could be drawn out without doing too much damage.

Then he built a device that he could insert into Henry's cheek and which would cover the arrowhead, so that it could be drawn out safely. He cleaned the wound with alcohol, in the form of white wine. Afterwards, he made a kind of ointment with a mixture of flour, barley and honey, and applied it to the prince's wound twice a day. Bradmore knew about the dangers of infection and also about tetanus, though he did not call it by that name. The prince remained at Kenilworth for several months, in too serious a condition to be moved.

If those cries of 'The King is dead' had been true and King Henry IV had died at the Battle of Shrewsbury, what would have become of the prince? One cannot help wondering. Under other circumstances, Henry IV's supporters would immediately have proclaimed his eldest son king, but if that son were hovering between life and death, it would have been unrealistic to do so. Hotspur's wife Elizabeth was the aunt of Richard II's heir presumptive, Edmund Mortimer, but Edmund was still a child. It is hard to say whether Hotspur had any designs on the throne for himself, but he would certainly have aspired to rule through his wife's young nephew if Henry IV had been removed from the scene. Bearing in mind the youth of Henry of Monmouth and the prior relationship between them, Hotspur might have spared the prince, whilst simultaneously nurturing a hope that he would never recover from his wound.

In July, while his son was recovering at Kenilworth, Henry IV is said to have made a pilgrimage to St Winifred's Well in Holywell, Flintshire, to give thanks both for his victory and for his son's survival. There remains some doubt as to whether his destination was actually Woolston in Shropshire, where there was another St Winifred's Well, possibly so named because the saint's relics had briefly rested there during the journey from North Wales to Shrewsbury.

The prince survived, as we know, but even though he was still a teenager, he must surely have been left with a sizeable scar. This may be the reason Henry's portraits show him in profile. Yet Bradmore recorded that the wound was in the left cheek, which is the one normally facing the viewer in near-contemporary portraits. Was this a double bluff, an attempt to disguise or deny the existence of a scar that anyone who had met him would have known about, perhaps in order to encourage any prospective royal bride? When, later, we read how Henry discouraged his subjects from looking him in the face, could it be that embarrassment rather than pride was the reason?

We have an image of Henry, reinforced by Shakespeare's play, as a handsome hero. On the contrary, he may actually have been quite horribly disfigured, which would have been no disadvantage to him as a soldier. It is easy to imagine what additional charisma it would have given him. No longer could anyone look at the sixteen-year-old prince and imagine he was going to be a pushover. Whether or not Henry V was shaped by his experience at Shrewsbury, he quickly developed as a military leader, and his father was able to hold onto the English throne largely because of this. After September 1403, King Henry IV never campaigned in Wales again. The young Earl of Chester imposed a curfew on the city and issued an order that any Welshman found out and about after hours would be executed (though there is no record of the penalty ever having been carried out) and it was he, Henry of Monmouth, who eventually defeated Owain Glyndŵr.

Chapter 4

Campaigning in Wales – Aberystwyth and Harlech

The seeds of Owain's failure were sown within his own rebellion; in Wales, it was harder to maintain power than it was to obtain it. Norman domination was such that Owain had never been as popular in South Wales as in his home area, and had only begun to make inroads in 1402. His English ally, Harry Hotspur, had been killed at Shrewsbury, but Hotspur's father was still on the warpath, along with Hotspur's brother-in-law, Edmund Mortimer, who, as a result of King Henry's slowness to ransom him after the Welsh captured him, had married Owain's daughter Catrin and changed sides.

Mortimer, as an uncle of the current Earl of March (who, at the age of fourteen, was still a royal ward, along with his younger brother), planned to snatch both nephews out of the king's hands, apparently with the collusion of Constance, Countess of Gloucester, a granddaughter of King Edward III. Constance's husband, the Earl of Gloucester, had been one of those involved in the Epiphany Rising, and she was thus not enamoured of King Henry IV. The Mortimer boys were in the line of succession to the throne of England – many would have said they were the rightful heirs – and would have been very useful to the rebels, but the plot failed and they were recaptured before they got as far as Wales. As for the countess, her property was confiscated and she was banished to Kenilworth Castle for safekeeping, where her path may have crossed that of Prince Henry. 'Mortimer's Tower' at Kenilworth is named for one of her ancestors.

Despite this setback, Owain did try to consolidate his rule in Wales, the more so as time went on. He was no youthful warrior, but a middle-aged man who had practised law, and his life experience caused him to realise that he could not hold Wales by force alone. Hence he spent part of the first decade of the fifteenth century making firm plans for the country's future, seeking buy-in to his ideas by calling parliaments at Machynlleth and Harlech. He attempted to maintain diplomatic relations with European power-brokers who might have an interest in supporting him against the English; these potential allies were to be found particularly in France and the Vatican. Was Henry of Monmouth observing these activities from Shrewsbury? Did the teenager recognise the wisdom of Owain's strategy and did he take the lesson in leadership, even before his own father trusted him with a share in the government of England? His later conquest of northern France would be notable for the methods he used to try to make English rule permanent.

Not surprisingly, the prince had spent a few months recuperating after the Battle of Shrewsbury, not returning to Wales until the following year, when he and his brother Thomas unsuccessfully attempted to raise Owain's siege on Coity Castle in the south, still hampered by a shortage of money to pay the troops. It is unrealistic to try to follow Henry's movements during the Welsh campaign in detail. He was not following particular routes as he would be when campaigning in France, but was mainly responding to attacks by Owain's forces and trying to gain strategic advantage by taking key strongholds. Thus it is hard to 'follow' in his footsteps in the truest sense.

The Normans had made considerable inroads into Wales well before Edward I's successful war against the princes of Gwynedd, but, in the south, their invasion had been relatively peaceful, with intermarriage between weak Welsh nobility and the powerful newcomers becoming almost the norm. One of Coity's first occupants was Sir Payn Turberville, one of the legendary 'Twelve Knights of Glamorgan', and the original castle was probably built before 1100. The Berkerolles family, who acquired it through marriage into the

Turberville dynasty in the thirteenth century, had transformed it. As a result of the improved defences, Sir Laurence Berkerolles, the owner of the castle at the turn of the fifteenth century, resisted Owain's onslaught for over a year, beginning in 1404.

Things were not going particularly well for Owain, as the castle was able to be reprovisioned by sea via the nearby River Ogmore. Berkerolles had, however, made an enemy of another local man, John Fleming, the deputy steward of the lordship of Ogmore, who decided to join the Welsh rebels and seems to have participated in the siege. Berkerolles was obliged to appeal to Parliament for assistance. It was in response to this plea that Henry and Thomas arrived on the scene in November 1404. Despite their intervention, the siege was not lifted for another ten months. In the years after Owain's rebellion, the castle would be extended and the defensive ditch and moat filled in. The castle is now a ruin and the surrounding area is largely built up, leaving little impression of what kind of an obstacle it presented to attacking forces.

In 1405, the same year he held his second parliament, Owain advanced into Herefordshire; there his forces, led by his capable lieutenant, Rhys Gethin, met with a smaller but better-organised army, sent by Prince Henry to intercept them. Commanding the royal force was John Talbot, who would one day be created Earl of Shrewsbury. The Talbots were a Marcher family with lands in Herefordshire, who had secured their position by intermarrying with the Welsh royal house of Dinefwr and by this time held Goodrich Castle. John Talbot was around the same age as Henry, but would live much longer and have an even more distinguished military career, earning himself nicknames like 'the English Achilles' and 'The Terror of the French' before being killed in battle in his sixties.

The battle between Talbot and Rhys Gethin took place at Grosmont, in Henry's native county of Monmouthshire, close to a castle where one of his great-grandfathers had been born nearly a century earlier, and the Welsh were driven back. Afterwards, the prince wrote from

Hereford, seeking his father's approval. He reports that 8,000 rebels had burned part of the town but that a relatively small number of his own men had seen them off. 'But true it is,' he writes, 'that the victory is not in the multitude of people, but in the might of the Lord.' This was a philosophy that would remain strong in him, especially after Agincourt.

Later that year, in another battle, known by the Welsh as Pwll Melyn and by the English as Usk, Henry of Monmouth commanded the English forces himself, while the opposition was led by Owain's eldest son, Gruffudd. Supporting Henry at Usk was his old friend the Earl of Warwick, and he was also fortunate in being able to make use of the local knowledge of loyalist Welshmen such as Dafydd Gam, who would later be at his side during the battle of Agincourt. At Pwll Melyn, Owain's brother Tudur was killed and his son was taken prisoner, along with several hundred others. Gruffudd spent the rest of his life in the Tower of London. A letter written by Henry IV at about this time reported that his own son was still in Wales, acting as a deputy for the king and delivering "chastisement" to the rebels.

It was in Henry of Monmouth's interests to defeat Owain, since the income he should have received from the principality of Wales was being severely reduced by the rebellion. Over the years he showed more awareness of economic issues than his father the king, and astutely set about improving his income by a combination of better management and military success. Thanks to his various titles – Prince of Wales, Duke of Cornwall, Duke of Lancaster and Earl of Chester – he was already a major landowner. By the time the opposition had been vanquished and the rebellion was over, he had improved his financial position five or six times over.

Even after Hotspur's death, Owain's alliance with Northumberland survived, and he was also getting help from overseas. In August, a French force arrived in West Wales to support Owain, but there was no direct confrontation between them and the English. The French, unable to locate the enemy and themselves short of money, returned home without any fighting having taken place. In the meantime, Prince Henry had shown an aptitude for gathering support from those with lands in the marches of Wales, such as the earls of Warwick and Arundel and his father's cousin, the Duke of York, who had an important logistical role in the Welsh campaign. He also picked out more humble individuals for advancement, thus gaining support where it was most valuable.

Initially, Henry of Monmouth's successes had been few, but his strategy of taking key castles and cutting off Glyndŵr's supply lines gradually bore fruit. By September 1407 the rebellion was grinding to a halt, and the prince set out to recapture Aberystwyth Castle, which had been in Owain's hands since 1404. Henry came with a substantial force of men, including the Duke of York, a seasoned campaigner, and it seemed unlikely that the small garrison could hold out. The royal party was well-equipped with cannon and siege engines.

The prince, now twenty years old, was essentially of a chivalrous nature, and thought it best to make a truce with Rhys Ddu ('Rhys the Black'), Owain's lieutenant, in order to avoid unnecessary bloodshed. He had not taken account of the fact that the occupying forces were mainly local men, and that there were others available to reinforce them when necessary. He had also failed to take account of Owain's contradictory personality, and he learned his lesson the hard way. A six-week pause in the hostilities was agreed, during which each side gave their word of honour not to add reinforcements.

When Owain received word from Rhys Ddu that the castle was to be given up to the English, far from accepting defeat, he hurried to the scene with a significant force, and Henry was forced to give up the attempt to take the castle. The setback was only temporary, however. The English returned a few months later, and this time took Aberystwyth without any difficulty, inflicting many casualties on the Welsh defenders. Now it was time for Henry of Monmouth to deal with Owain's stronghold of Harlech Castle, which was already under siege.

We know that Henry did not spend the entirety of his time in Wales during the years of the uprising. Specifically, in the early summer of 1406, Parliament twice requested that he station himself there permanently, revealing that he was not always present to supervise the campaign against Glyndŵr in person. By this time the rebellion had been going on for six years and it was to be some years more before Henry's rival was finally defeated. However, the prince's ambitions went beyond being his father's 'lieutenant'.

In 1408, between the sieges of Aberystwyth and Harlech, the prince took time out to make a pilgrimage to Yorkshire, where he visited the shrines of St John of Beverley (an eighth-century bishop) and St John of Bridlington, a monk named John Twenge who had died less than thirty years earlier. Henry seems to have been taking a leaf out of his father's book, invoking his Christian faith as a way of obtaining God's favour in the war against the rebels. If that is the case, he must soon have felt that his faith was vindicated. He would later credit both saints with having a hand in his victory at Agincourt.

*****

During the period of Owain Glyndŵr's ascendancy, Harlech became his seat of government as well as his family home, and was the location for a parliament in 1405. Owain had captured Harlech Castle in 1404, at around the same as Aberystwyth, but Harlech was a far more daunting prospect for anyone hoping to re-take it for the king. Whereas the castle at Aberystwyth had been rebuilt on a twelfth-century plan and was already falling into disrepair, Harlech had been built by King Edward I during his conquest of Wales in the 1280s, on a high rock overlooking the Irish Sea; it remains impressive even though it is now a ruin.

Visitors may be surprised to find that the cliff on which the castle stands is no longer on the coast. A golf course, caravan park and railway line can now be found on land that was once part of Tremadog

Bay. The water-gate and 100-plus steps leading down to it are still to be seen; by this means, past inhabitants of the castle were able to supply it from the sea. In 2015, the original drawbridge, long since gone, was replaced with a 'floating' footbridge, allowing pedestrian access via the main entrance for the first time in centuries. This was part of a major refurbishment project which vastly improved visitor facilities at the castle.

*****

Henry of Monmouth's troops laid siege to Harlech Castle, employing cannon brought from Bristol and previously used, with limited success, at Aberystwyth. His use of gunnery, a relatively new resource, combined with existing artillery such as siege engines, would become a notable feature of his military career. To Aberystwyth, Henry had brought 'Messager', a brass cannon weighing around two metric tonnes, and 'Neelpot' (perhaps a corruption of 'Nieuwport'), an iron cannon. Both had been broken or exploded during the siege. At Harlech, another large iron cannon, 'The King's Daughter', exploded. Nevertheless, the power of the guns contributed significantly to the success of his attack on Harlech.

Henry's forces effectively finished the job of quashing the rebellion by taking Owain's family prisoner, the task made easier by the death of Owain's son-in-law, Edmund Mortimer, in January 1409, 'reduced to great distress'. The exact cause and date of Mortimer's death are uncertain; it may have been the result of plague, starvation or a wound. Henry was probably not on the spot when the castle fell, having returned to take Aberystwyth, leaving the immensely capable John Talbot in charge of the other siege.

Owain's wife and children were captured following the taking of Harlech, but Owain himself was not there when the English got inside. Most of the family ended their lives in the Tower of London, but Henry was never to capture Owain, who was allowed to disappear.

John Cowper Powys, in his fanciful 1941 novel, *Owen Glendower*, suggests that Henry and Owain were well known to one another as a result both of Henry's time in Wales as a boy and of Owain's military service under both Richard II and Bolingbroke; this seems unlikely, but it is not impossible that they had met. Henry may well have taken a conscious decision not to go after Owain because there was nothing to be gained by it; he may have believed that, like terrorists in today's society, the Welshman had so many followers that his execution would have created a martyr in whose memory further rebels would be spurred into action. Meanwhile, he continued to hold onto Owain's family as a bargaining counter. Nevertheless, Glyndŵr, by allying himself with the French, had given Henry an excuse for his eventual invasion of France.

The Seat of Power

Even before the fall of Harlech, Henry of Monmouth was beginning to strain at his father's leash. By the end of 1406, he had a place on the royal council. Any desire Parliament might have had to see him spend more time in Wales went by the board as his father's health became more and more suspect. The prince was obliged to attend council meetings in London and other locations, and he appears to have relished the opportunity to display his skills as an administrator. Whispers of a regency began to circulate.

The prince was soon making financial grants to his friends and supporters, gradually building up a following of his own to rival his father's. His circle included the Earl of Arundel, who was close to Henry Beaufort, as well as the Earl of Warwick and Richard Courtenay, later Bishop of Norwich and the king's chief intelligence-gatherer. The Archbishop of Canterbury, Thomas Arundel, though related to the Earl of Arundel, did not enjoy the prince's favour, and this may have been one of the reasons for the archbishop's resignation from his secondary post as Lord Chancellor in 1410.

One of those who may have benefited from his previous associations with the Prince of Wales was Thomas Montagu, the son of Maud, Countess of Salisbury, one of Henry's guardians during his childhood at Courtfield. Maud's husband had been executed for treason, but in 1409, his eldest surviving son would be restored to his father's title and estates. No doubt this was a reward to the countess for the care she had previously taken of the king's vulnerable young son. Thomas Montagu would go on to earn a military reputation fighting alongside the prince and would follow him faithfully to Agincourt.

Because of his father's poor health, Henry of Monmouth was practically ruling the country by 1410, having spent most of the first decade of the fifteenth century putting down the revolt in Wales. In 1409 he became constable of Dover Castle and warden of the Cinque Ports, and in 1410 he was Captain of Calais. This did not mean he was obliged to be physically present in any of these places, but records show that he claimed operational expenses for the defence of Calais. In 1410 his father also gave him an estate in Coldharbour, within the City of London, and he often spent time there. The manor house no longer exists, having been destroyed in the Great Fire of London in 1666. Its location was close to the present-day Cannon Street railway station.

On the surface, relations were good. However, there were still tensions between the prince and his father, and meanwhile he had also fallen out with his younger brother, Thomas of Lancaster, who had always been their father's favourite and was by now well on the path to success as a military leader. Their father, in what should have been the prime of his life, was suffering from a mystery disease. Some said it was leprosy; some said it was what we would now call a sexually-transmitted disease. Some said it was a curse, brought on by his decision to execute the rebel Archbishop of York in 1405. Whatever the disease was, it was killing King Henry IV, slowly but inexorably.

The king's eldest son had lost interest in pleasing him, and this period was his window of opportunity. However, having disagreed with his father on a number of policy issues and exceeded his authority on more than one occasion, the Prince of Wales was removed from the royal council when the king's health temporarily improved towards the end of 1411. He had already done his duty by his father in putting down Glyndŵr's rebellion. Now he was back in London, it was time to let his hair down. With the king in no position to control his activities, this may have been the period when Prince Hal got the reputation that we associate with him. He and his young followers, including some of his brothers, were said to have roistered and doistered at will. One of the two fifteenth-century 'lives' of Henry V describes him as 'the fervent soldier of Venus as well as Mars', suggesting an excess of sexual activity. Records of expenditure on medicine for the prince in these years *could* be interpreted as meaning that he too had a brush with a sexually-transmitted disease.

Whatever his youthful failings, the king could hardly disinherit the Prince of Wales, who was both the heir to the Lancastrian dynasty and a popular young man. Adam of Usk, who had for a time tacitly supported the Glyndwr rebellion, returned from exile in 1408 seeking to find his way back into the king's good books; he referred to the prince as 'a youth upright and filled with virtues and wisdom'. Adam also admired Henry's devotion to God, calling him 'the brave champion of the faith who was filled with most Christian zeal'. (Later, tired of watching the members of his congregation struggling under the burden of taxation, he would seem to have 'gone off' the king.)

Henry IV punished his wayward son by refusing to allow him to lead an expedition to Aquitaine that had been planned for 1412, particularly galling for the prince since one of the titles that went with that of Prince of Wales was Prince of Aquitaine. Aquitaine was one of England's oldest possessions in France. It was where the Black Prince had spent much of his career and where King Richard II had been born, and was one of the many parts of his future dominion that the prince had not had the opportunity to visit. This was not the only one of the English king's French possessions that was under threat, and sooner or later a war in France was almost inevitable. The king's rejection of his eldest son was the last straw in the breakdown of their relationship, especially when Henry's brother Thomas was allowed to take his place as head of the expedition.

For the time being, Thomas's campaign was not exactly a triumph but did allow the English to access their possessions. Since 1404 the French had been attempting to retake Aquitaine, on and off, and Thomas had been appointed Captain of Guyenne (the French name for the province), but had never been there before. The purpose of the campaign was to defend England's right to the principality and to support the Armagnac dukes, including Orléans, with whom Henry IV had a mutual support agreement. Prince Henry had favoured an alliance with Burgundy, but Thomas settled with the Armagnac faction in order to obtain recognition of England's possession of Aquitaine. He also managed to exact a financial settlement from the French, but did not cover himself in glory when he allowed his men to pillage on their way home. Henry was obliged to swear to uphold the terms of the Treaty of Bourges, even though he mistrusted his new allies.

The Prince of Wales responded to his father's rejection by retreating to his manor of Cheylesmore in Cheshire, now a suburb of Coventry. This manor house was traditionally associated with the royal family. Richard II had stayed there, as had his father, the Black Prince. A small part of the fourteenth-century building remains in use today as the local register office, the rest having been demolished in 1955. It was from this location that the prince wrote a letter attempting to dispel certain rumours that were current, to the effect that he was planning a coup against his father. According to him, 'sons of iniquity' were responsible for the rumours. His action did not convince everyone. His friend Henry Beaufort, who was deeply implicated in the supposed coup, found himself in disgrace and was removed from his role in government.

However, shortly after writing his letter, Henry marched down to London with his retainers, for a meeting with his father, who was now in such poor health that he could not walk. Some chroniclers claimed that the prince arrived wearing the old scholar's gown he had used while a student at Oxford (it surely would have been a far-from-perfect fit by this time) and, kneeling before his father, offered him a dagger with which to kill him if he had ever given any cause for suspicions of disloyalty. A meeting certainly took place, but, whatever its true nature, it failed to achieve anything of importance. There was no time left for a meaningful reconciliation.

Chapter 5

Early Kingship – Kenilworth and other Royal Residences

Accession to the throne

In March 1413, Henry IV died, aged only forty-six. He had already decided to be buried at Canterbury Cathedral, but the location he specified was not the position where his effigy is now located, close to that of the Black Prince. It has been suggested that the tomb already prepared for Archbishop Thomas Arundel was used to house the king, since Arundel's remains were subsequently located under the nave of the cathedral, and Arundel's own tomb, constructed later, has no effigy.

Henry V's coronation took place about three weeks later, on 9 April, and by all accounts was a bizarre occasion. There was a hailstorm while the young king was processing from the Tower of London to Westminster Abbey, and snow continued to fall for a further two days. We choose to think of extreme weather as a modern phenomenon, but England and Wales endured it for much of that year. In the summer, extreme heat caused forest fires and triggered outbreaks of disease, whilst harvests were adversely affected by autumn storms. There were murmurings that these were ill omens, perhaps a sign of God's displeasure in that the sons of the House of Lancaster were not the true heirs to the throne.

One of the first things the new king did was to bring the body of the former king, Richard II, from its resting place at Kings Langley in Hertfordshire to Westminster Abbey, where Richard had planned to be buried alongside his first wife. The action may have been prompted by the trial, in July 1413, of a man named John Whitelock, a rebel who claimed that King Richard was still alive. Whitelock was accused of conspiring with the Scots to overthrow King Henry V, but he escaped from custody before the verdict could be passed. Silencing this particular rebel was not, however, Henry's only motive in re-burying Richard II. He was showing respect for the late monarch, not only because of their personal relationship but because his father was a usurper, and the re-interment was a kind of penance, a way of showing that Henry V was not to be blamed for the sins of Henry IV. The young king was already turning over a new leaf. Perhaps, having known all along that it was only a matter of time before he ascended the throne, he had been sowing his wild oats while he got the chance. After his accession, he became notoriously chaste and pious. But he didn't become peace-loving.

Further amends were made by releasing the now-adult Edmund Mortimer, Earl of March, and his younger brother Roger, from the captivity into which they had been placed by King Henry IV nearly ten years earlier. As Prince of Wales, Henry had long been their custodian and had treated them far more leniently than his father would have done. They did, strictly speaking, have a better claim to the throne than he did, but he appears not to have held that against them. Now, in an effort to ensure their future loyalty, he knighted them both.

These were not the only prisoners Henry's father had been holding. Murdoch Stewart, son of the Duke of Albany, had been taken in battle in 1402. His father had been Scotland's regent since the death of King Robert III in 1406, whilst the country's nominal king, nineteen-year-old James I, was a prisoner in England. In this case, however, Henry was initially less lenient than his father. Henry IV had allowed the boy king to become part of his household, but Henry V now transferred him to the Tower of London, where he was held along with his cousin Murdoch. James would have a long time to wait for his freedom, and it was Murdoch who was released in 1416, in exchange for twenty-one-year-old Henry Percy, the son of Henry's old mentor Harry Hotspur. Young Percy had been held hostage in Scotland since the death of his grandfather in 1408, and the fact that he had a claim on the English throne through his Mortimer mother may have been one of the reasons he had not been ransomed; in releasing him, Henry was not only showing that he did not fear Percy as a rival but also putting trust in his loyalty as the son of Hotspur. On his return home, Percy was restored to the earldom of Northumberland, and became a reliable supporter of the Lancastrian dynasty throughout Henry's reign and afterwards.

There seems little doubt that Henry V had absorbed the best of the advice his father was capable of giving him and had improved on it with the wisdom that his own experiences had added. He was not an absolute monarch; any attempt to become one would quickly have condemned him to the same fate as his uncle, King Richard II. The Lancastrian dynasty was not yet fully accepted, and there was still unrest in parts of England. In Cirencester, where the weavers' guild was strong, the abbot arrested certain individuals who had failed to pay local taxes or customs duties. This resulted in riots, and the case went to court. Parliament demanded tough and immediate action, but the king pardoned those who had been sentenced for their part in the violence, with the consent of the abbot.

In general, the English parliament would give Henry far less trouble than it had given his father. This was partly because his grasp on the throne was seen to be more secure than his father's. The Lancaster dynasty was becoming firmly established. More than this, though, Henry was a different personality from his father, and always had one eye on the need to cooperate and compromise with the people who held the purse strings. A long-standing bugbear with parliament had been Henry IV's failure to enforce law and order. Henry V tackled this problem with energy, taking his leading enforcers home to Leicester Castle with him to work out a strategy. It would take time but, had he lived longer, it is impossible to imagine that he would not eventually have succeeded.

Up to a point, the very process of taking a large army out of the country could be seen as a contribution to the preservation of peace at home.

Another of Henry's first tasks as king was to deal with heresy, and here he would prove less compassionate with offenders. The Lollards, followers of John Wycliffe, had first appeared more than thirty years earlier. John of Gaunt had been their protector, and while Prince of Wales Henry had declined to do anything about a supposed Lollard cell within Oxford University. He had tried desperately to obtain the recantation of a Lollard named John Badby, even intervening while Badby was being burned at the stake to offer him mercy. Henry's concern was for Badby's soul as well as his life, but he did not hesitate to allow the burning to continue when Badby rejected his offer.

Wycliffe was long since dead, but the Lollard movement still had its leaders, and these included Sir John Oldcastle, a veteran who had held the castles of Builth and Kidwelly on Henry's behalf during the Glyndŵr revolt; if Oldcastle has sometimes been seen as a model for Falstaff, it is not for his want of physical courage. After the putting-down of the rebellion, he had been sent overseas to support the Burgundians against the French king.

As Prince of Wales, Henry considered Oldcastle one of his most trustworthy supporters, and he must have been horrified when the middle-aged knight was accused of heresy in 1413, as a result of having allowed the churches on his lands to be a venue for unlicensed preaching. When the new king acceded to the throne, he was willing to overlook Sir John's carelessness in being caught with a heretical text in his possession, and hoped to talk him round. Oldcastle was placed in the Tower of London, and was allowed forty days in which to renounce his heretical views.

Henry elected to spend his first Christmas as king at Eltham Palace, which had been one of his father's favourite residences. The palace had been a gift to his ancestor, King Edward II, from an obsequious bishop, and was reputedly the place where Edward III had famously dismissed gossip while dancing with a courtier's wife, resulting in the foundation of the Order of the Garter. For years to come it would be a regular venue for the monarchy's Christmas festivities. Its main drawback as a royal residence was its location, miles to the south-east of Westminster and some distance from the river. The building now open to the public and in the care of English Heritage is much altered, but incorporates part of the medieval structure.

It was at this point that Sir John Oldcastle, who had escaped from the Tower, raised a minor rebellion; some said he intended the king's death, and the rebels planned to act during the Twelfth Night celebrations. Lollards came from around the country to Oldcastle's aid, but the king got wind of this and moved his household to Westminster, ordering the city gates to be closed. In the end, only eighty men were captured when the king's forces arrived on the scene, led by the stalwart Earl of Warwick. Almost all were put to death, some by burning at the stake, but once again Oldcastle escaped, and it would be another three years before he was brought to justice. Sir Roger Acton, who had also previously enjoyed royal favour, was less fortunate, and was strung up at Tyburn for his treachery.

In the meantime, Henry exacted appropriate penalties on the Lollard community in England, forcing the remaining heretics underground. The 'Statute of Lollards', passed by his parliament at Leicester in 1414, ensured that harsh new instructions on dealing with the sect were passed down the chain of command. Parliament would congratulate him regularly on taking this hard line for years to come. Henry was developing a long-term spiritual vision for the success of his reign. Warwick, who seems to have shared this vision and had already spent two years on a pilgrimage to the Holy Land, was rewarded for his support by being made Captain of Calais.

The King's Great Work

Early in his reign, Henry endowed a convent of the Bridgettine order at Syon Abbey, the Augustinian monastery of St Saviour and

St Bridget of Syon. This was part of his 'Great Work', a series of projects designed to emphasise his religious devotion and be a lasting reminder of his power as a monarch. Money for building projects was always easier to find in peacetime. The construction work cost at least £10,000. The king laid the foundation stone in person on 22 February 1415, with Richard Clifford, Bishop of London, in attendance.

His motivation was at least partly to obtain God's blessing for the coming invasion of France, for which he was already making preparations, and he was clearly influenced in this by his chancellor, Henry Beaufort. He had notified some of London's most important citizens of his intentions, in a shameless plea for the cash to fund the expedition, referring to 'God our rewarder' in his speech. He was assembling a fleet and he did not want to leave it entirely up to God to find him the money. One of those who helped out financially was the wealthy merchant Richard ('Dick') Whittington, who had retained his position as Lord Mayor of London by supporting the Lancastrian coup of 1399.

As confessor at Syon Abbey, Henry chose William Alnwick, later Bishop of Norwich and Lincoln, whom he had first met just before his accession, having supposedly chosen to confess his sins to Alnwick – then a hermit-priest at Westminster Abbey – on the night of his father's death. Alnwick was a relentless campaigner against heresy and a scourge of the Lollards. It was in the same year, 1415, that Jan Hus, the Bohemian-born proto-Protestant leader, was burned at the stake in Germany, leading to a series of religious wars that would engulf parts of Europe in the latter years of Henry's reign and after.

Elsewhere in the area of what is now Isleworth, Henry founded two more religious houses. One, a monastery of the Celestine order, was occupied by French monks who, ironically, declined to pray for Henry's military success; the monastery was quickly broken up, and the occupants of Syon Abbey moved in to replace them. The site of the second Syon Abbey has been excavated in recent years, and findings initially suggested that it was one of England's biggest. Subsequent archaeological work has established that it was not as large as first thought, but a proportion of the foundations is hidden under newer buildings. Since it was the only Bridgettine convent in England, the investigation has sought out contemporary Bridgettine buildings in other countries that may throw light on its original appearance and layout. Following its destruction during the reformation, it was replaced with a Georgian mansion, now called Syon House, but the foundations of the abbey were located by archaeologists and confirmed its location. *Time Team* produced a fascinating digital reconstruction of the abbey, but the later excavations resulted in discoveries that altered these conclusions.

The other religious house established by Henry V was the House of Jesus of Bethlehem of Sheen (often spelt Shene), a Carthusian establishment, also known as Sheen Priory. A sixteenth-century drawing of the priory survives, as a detail in sketches of Richmond Palace (formerly Sheen Palace) by the Flemish artist Anton van den Wyngaerde, who worked throughout northern Europe. Wyngaerde helpfully marks it 'Cien' on his drawings. There are no remains visible above ground, and whatever may survive now lies beneath the Royal Mid-Surrey Golf Course. We may, however, suppose that Syon Abbey was similar in design, since the excavations by a team from Birkbeck College, London, revealed that Syon, too, had a tower. The young King James of Scotland seems to have been impressed by his captor's architectural ambitions; when he eventually returned to take up his throne, he too would found a Carthusian monastery, at Perth, where he would be buried.

Sheen Palace, renamed Richmond Palace during a later reign, had been a favourite residence of King Richard II and his first wife, Anne of Bohemia. Richard fell out of love with it after Anne died there in 1394 – within three days of Henry's mother Mary's death in Peterborough – and it was now in need of renovation. Henry began work on it in 1414, envisaging a defensive structure with two towers; these, and a new chapel, had been completed by the time of his death. He built over the gardens of the old palace, importing building materials from Calais and Rouen as well as from more distant parts of England, but created a private garden and orchard, as well as private lodgings for himself. Temporary buildings were constructed out of timbers that had originally formed part of his manor at Byfleet in Surrey (not the same Byfleet Manor that can be seen today); these were the on-site accommodation for the builders, the portakabins of their day. However, Henry's plans were frequently interrupted and the palace remained half-built at the time of his death. It was another twenty years before his son took on responsibility for its completion.

Sheen Palace had to be almost entirely rebuilt by one of Henry's successors, King Henry VII, following a disastrous fire later in the century, which destroyed most of what Henry V had created. Even that third building no longer stands, having suffered irreparable damage during the English Civil Wars in the seventeenth century. The converted gatehouse ('Trumpeters' House'), which can still be seen, originates from around 1500, but its present appearance dates from about 1710. Although now in private hands, the garden is occasionally opened to the public on special occasions and for charity events.

Henry did not need another London home, since he had his own apartments closer to the centre of administration, at Westminster Palace, a huge complex that was destroyed by fire in the nineteenth century. Before his accession, the king had occupied apartments in the 'Prince's Palace', a section of the complex which is believed to have gained its name as a result of being used as a residence by earlier princes such as Richard, Earl of Cornwall, a younger son of King John. He continued to live in fairly simple style, surrounded by luxury he did not particularly prize. There are records of the fine tapestries that adorned the royal apartments and even the curtains on the royal bed. A private chapel was conveniently situated next to his bedchamber. Much of the administration of the realm was carried out from offices located within a stone's throw of the king's suite.

It is harder to find fair assessments of Henry V as a king than it is to find descriptions of his prowess as a military leader. Commentators have seen him as everything from a despot to a wise and practical administrator. One fifteenth-century account describes how, after dinner, on days 'when full royal estate was not kept', he would lean upon a cushion laid on top of a cupboard and hear petitions from his subjects. This gives us an impression of informality that is altogether out of keeping with the contrasting pictures of a king so haughty that he would not allow anyone to look him in the face. However, it may give the false impression that it was normal for the king to deal with such matters in person, which is far from the truth. A number of clerks were employed to handle the various petitions, depending on their type, and to carry out the king's wishes.

Another occupant of Westminster Palace at this time was Joanna of Navarre, Henry's stepmother, the widow of King Henry IV. Now in her mid-forties, she had children from her first marriage, most of them younger than her stepson but nevertheless mature enough to be left in France, so there was no rivalry for her affections. Henry V and his brothers are said to have had a good relationship with her, but it deteriorated after Agincourt, as will be seen.

When Henry wanted to be close to London but far enough away to be able to avoid crowds, there was always Windsor Castle, though it was not a great favourite with him. The changes made at Windsor by his great-grandfather, Edward III, were remarkable, resulting in a palace complex that inspired several other great buildings of the fourteenth and fifteenth centuries. The tradition of communal living that had been thought nothing of in earlier centuries was going out of fashion, as could be seen by the transformation of Windsor. The castle had become a status symbol, copied not only by Edward's son John of Gaunt (at Kenilworth) but also by King Charles V of France when he built the castle of Vincennes and remodelled the Louvre in Paris.

*****

We have already touched on Henry's acquaintance with Kenilworth Castle, around thirty miles from Leicester, where his wound was treated by Bradmore after the Battle of Shrewsbury, and he returned there many times. Kenilworth was another possession of the Dukes of Lancaster, acquired by John of Gaunt through his marriage to Blanche. In 1371, a few years after Blanche's death in 1368, Gaunt married Constance of Castile, an alliance that enabled him to claim the throne of Castile and begin behaving like a king – a claim he was eventually obliged to relinquish in 1388.

During the 1380s and 1390s, Gaunt had made many improvements to the fabric of Kenilworth Castle, as well as extending it to include an additional tower, new kitchens, new apartments and a new, bigger great hall for gatherings. Thus it had been the most comfortable place possible for Gaunt's grandson to recover, even though this meant a journey of over sixty miles from the battlefield. The 'great mere' surrounding the castle had a defensive purpose but also added to the imposing appearance of the structure. Henry would become fond of Kenilworth and would build his own private residence there.

Kenilworth is still an impressive sight, even in its ruined state. A later Earl of Leicester, the favourite of Queen Elizabeth I, turned it into a grand residence in order to impress his queen, adding a gatehouse and tower and the range of rooms called 'Leicester's Building'. Nevertheless, the excellence of John of Gaunt's great hall is clear from what can still be seen of it, including the Gothic windows restored in the nineteenth century. The hall had six fireplaces and the biggest roof in England after the one at Westminster Palace.

Gaunt had the biggest household of anyone except the King of England, with nearly a hundred knights, and even a few aristocrats, permanently at his service. Moreover, Kenilworth was only one of his many properties. Many court occasions must have been held in the great hall during the reigns of Gaunt's son and grandson. Gaunt also created the Oriel, for more private entertaining, and the 'Strong Tower', with its stone vaulting, is another example of his work.

'Lunn's Tower', probably named after the River Lune in Lancashire and attributed by some to Gaunt, was partly rebuilt in the 1870s and would have been higher at the time of Henry's residence.

The Pleasance in the Marsh

In 1414, at around the same time as he authorised the start of work on Sheen Palace, Henry V began building a personal retreat, a banqueting house named 'The Pleasance in the Marsh', at Kenilworth. It seems that Henry conceived the idea while staying at Kenilworth during the season of Lent in 1414; this time of self-denial and religious contemplation might have caused him to recognise the need for a space in which to be himself and enjoy a little peace and quiet. The new building was constructed on a four-acre site a short distance from the castle, on the far side of the great mere. The mere no longer exists, although plans to recreate it have been mooted; should this happen, the original spectacular landscape would be restored to how it looked in Henry's day, and would help to explain the reason he chose this particular spot when he wanted privacy. He and his visitors would approach The Pleasance by boat, landing at a small private wooden jetty and crossing a bridge over a double moat to the artificial island where the building stood. This wide moat represented a secondary barrier, for the purpose of discouraging uninvited guests.

The Pleasance, completed in about 1417, was built mostly of timber but with substantial stone foundations. It had a small tower at each of its four corners, as well as an internal courtyard and garden where the young king could enjoy seclusion. The remaining earthworks, clearly delineating the form of the island and moat, as well as the position of the private harbour, can still be seen, even though the house itself was demolished during the reign of King Henry VIII. Nowadays the location is on private land, but can be reached by a public footpath enabling it to be visited separately from the castle.

Building it would not have been straightforward. Apart from the need for some draining of marshland, one of Henry's biographers, Thomas Elmham, stated that there was a heavily-overgrown area, popular with foxes, to be cleared first. Elmham describes the building as a 'viridarium' or pleasure garden, and draws a simplistic parallel between the foxes which had to be chased off the land and the French with their 'foxy' ways. Archaeologists have discovered evidence for the central garden and courtyard. Although most of the building was of wood, the bases of the four stone corner towers have also been found, and the location of the kitchens has been tentatively identified. There is a record of one Roger Castle being paid for timber to be used in the construction of a 'chamber in the water under Kenilworth Castle'.

The word 'pleasance', in this case, is roughly synonymous with pleasure, and this was the purpose of Henry's private palace, 'le plesans en marais', but this does not necessarily refer to pleasures of the flesh, since Henry was notoriously abstemious after his accession to the throne. In addition to banqueting and entertaining selected guests, it might have been used for hunting parties, but Henry seems to have used it as a place to get away from it all.

After his successful second French campaign, grateful for the assistance of the Scottish king in helping to neutralise the opposition, Henry invited King James (still nominally a prisoner of the English Crown), with the English noblewoman he hoped to marry, to go on a progress with him. In the course of this, they visited Kenilworth and were entertained at The Pleasance. Unfortunately, a further outbreak of resistance by the French, supported by some Scots, would put paid to James's hopes of being allowed to return to his own country for another year or two. He would not be released until after Henry's death.

Chapter 6

The Road to Agincourt

The Battle of Agincourt, which took place on 25 October 1415, is an event whose significance has been thoroughly misrepresented by the media in the 600 years since it happened. A lot of what the average person knows about Agincourt and its main protagonist, King Henry V of England, has been gleaned from the works of William Shakespeare Much of that will be correct. However, we have come to expect too much of Shakespeare, who was using sources copied from earlier sources and embroidered on. To make matters worse, some modern productions of *Henry V* gloss over or completely omit scenes that show the hero's less attractive side. We need to look at our knowledge of history critically and recognise the gaps in it and the areas where we may have been misled. We may never be able to find out for certain what happened at Agincourt but we can at least try to establish which parts are fact and which are speculation or fantasy.

What most people will definitely already know about Agincourt is that the battle was fought between the English and the French. Most readers will not be particularly familiar with the actual events of 1415 except through the Shakespeare play, which has been brought to the screen several times, most notably by Laurence Olivier in 1944 and Kenneth Branagh in 1989. Both of these versions have their merits, but both contain historical inaccuracies over and above those introduced into the story by Shakespeare. For example, the Olivier version shows the English cavalry charging across an enormously wide, grassy field, which did not happen, whilst the Branagh version shows the king going bareheaded to attack the walls of Harfleur, which he would certainly not have done, especially after his experiences at the Battle of Shrewsbury. We must learn to recognise artistic licence when we see it.

Shakespeare portrays Henry as a real golden boy, a tough and rebellious (but fun-loving) teenager who turns almost overnight into a strong, just ruler and a magnificent battle commander. Historical research may, alternatively, suggest that he was neither a particular tearaway in his early youth nor a born military commander, nor, in fact, a very likeable person. Some historians have suggested that he was a misogynist, and he certainly gained a reputation for brutality in his dealings with the French, a reputation he shared with the Black Prince before him. In spite of this, he is remembered by history as a 'good' king. Even the Welsh, not normally fans of the medieval English monarchy, are rather proud of the fact that he was born in Monmouth. However, his posthumous reputation rests almost entirely on his miraculous victory at the Battle of Agincourt, and this does him no favours.

With Wales, Ireland, the Scottish borders and England's French possessions all in danger from violent incursions, Henry was obliged to do something to show rival monarchs that he was a power to be reckoned with. The Hundred Years' War, of which Agincourt was part, had been one of early successes for England, but by the time Henry set sail from Southampton, it was over sixty years since the English had won a significant victory over the French. The achievements of his predecessor, the Black Prince, were all but forgotten.

When it came to fighting wars in France, the king's experiences in Wales were invaluable. His decision to recruit Welshmen to his army, so soon after a rebellion that had almost cost his father the throne, was a brave one, and leads us to believe that he had observed their skills at first hand. The Black Prince had been Prince of Wales before Henry, and, because of the extent of his Welsh lands, he had been one of the first English leaders to recruit Welsh archers. When he did so, he gave them a green-and-white uniform. The main reason he needed to give them a distinguishing feature was the fact that many of them spoke no English and the rest of his army might have mistaken them for the enemy. These Welsh archers had done good service at battles like Crécy and Poitiers, about seventy years before Agincourt, and they were now wielding a bow that was more powerful and arrows that had developed so that they were capable of piercing armour.

The names of soldiers recruited in Wales for Henry's invasion of France are recorded in muster rolls of June 1415 from Carmarthen and Brecon; the latter town was an administrative centre for the duchy of Lancaster (which Henry had inherited from his father). They included a few men-at-arms, a few mounted archers and nearly 500 foot archers all told. A much smaller number were recruited at Kidwelly. Some of the men may have been retained for home defence purposes, but most travelled to Hereford and thence to Southampton, to embark for France. Their passage through Warminster, Wiltshire, is recorded, with locals complaining about their conduct. Nevertheless, those Welshmen who had been involved in the rebellion of Owain Glyndŵr could reasonably have hoped that their subsequent service to the king would result in a pardon or even a more tangible reward.

In 2015, as part of the celebration of the 600th anniversary of the Battle of Agincourt, an 'Agincourt Wales Trail' was devised as a visitor attraction. Most of the locations on the trail have little to do with the battle itself. It begins at Trecastle near Brecon, and continues through the city of Brecon itself to Tretower, where the castle was a stronghold of Henry IV during the revolt of Owain Glyndŵr. Near here, in 1404, Richard Beauchamp, Earl of Warwick, successfully engaged Owain's forces in battle. The trail then passes through Abergavenny, where William ap Thomas (the 'Blue Knight of Gwent'), and his wife Gwladys – the daughter of the loyal Dafydd Gam – are buried at the priory, to reach Raglan Castle, their former home. After Monmouth, the trail turns south, passing through the village of St Briavels in the Forest of Dean, where a small royal castle of the twelfth century has been converted to a youth hostel; it remains in the care of English Heritage and is open to the public. Its owner, the Duke of Gloucester, was dispossessed and executed following the Epiphany Rising, and it became the property of Henry's younger brother John. Finally, the trail reaches Caldicot, back in Monmouthshire, where the extensive and well-preserved castle was a favourite haunt of King Richard II. It subsequently became part of the Duchy of Lancaster and eventually passed to Henry V's widow, Catherine of Valois.

An army is said to march on its stomach. Perhaps Henry did not intend that his fighting men should do a lot of marching, but they still needed to live, and there were contracts for supplies, such as meat from Titchfield Abbey in Hampshire, one of the places where Henry stayed overnight on his way to Southampton. He also had permanent, official sources of certain essentials, such as weapons. The Tower of London was England's central arsenal and armoury, and nearby Ludgate was a centre for the manufacture of bows and arrows. Legislation had already been passed to ensure that these were made to a high standard. In spite of all these preparations, Henry did not have the resources he would have needed for a lengthy invasion of northern France. His military experience was enough for him to have been aware of this, yet he could not have been anticipating anything like what actually happened.

Our nationalistic side leads us to believe that the English were somehow 'in the right' against the French. (Thomas Elmham would later claim that St George had actually been seen fighting on the English side at Agincourt!) England and France had been at war, on and off, since 1337. At the root of the conflict was the English monarch's claim to the French throne. When Philippe IV's three sons all died in turn and the family ran out of male heirs, the next in line for the throne should logically have been Edward III, who was the son of Philippe's daughter, Isabella. Instead, the Valois dynasty, through a nephew of Philippe's, ensured that the throne did not pass to the English king by appealing to the 'Salic law', an ancient Frankish legal code that they had never been too bothered about previously. Under Salic law, not only could a woman not inherit the throne, her son could not inherit it through her.

Shakespeare explains this situation quite well for the benefit of his audience early in his play, in a scene where Henry consults his own legal advisers about the rightfulness of his claim to the French throne. Although the French had the Pope on their side, they also had massive problems because their latest Valois king, Charles VI, was mentally ill, and this had resulted in bitter rivalry among the French nobility, specifically the Armagnac and Orléans families, not to mention the Burgundians. Ironically, Henry V's father, Bolingbroke, had been a beneficiary of these internal divisions, choosing Paris as his place of exile when he was banished from the kingdom by his cousin, Richard II. There he had been welcomed by the King of France, Charles VI, even though the latter was also Richard's father-in-law.

At the point when Henry launched his invasion of France, the two countries had been at peace, albeit sometimes an uneasy one, for twenty-five years. No one could reasonably have expected the French to give up their position on the rights of succession. Charles VI had a son, the Dauphin Louis, but he was actually the third of Charles's sons to hold that title, as two earlier sons had already died in childhood. So, after Bolingbroke took the throne of England, there could have been a reasonable expectation that, at some future date, the French throne could pass to his heirs in due course, provided that the French relaxed their view on the Salic Law. However, one of Bolingbroke's close allies, Louis, Duke of Orléans, a brother of King Charles VI, was disgusted when he usurped the English throne, and henceforth was hostile to the English. This malign influence was reduced when the duke was assassinated by Burgundians in 1407, his son and successor being only in his early teens.

Unlike his predecessors, the Dauphin Louis grew up and, by the time of Agincourt, he was about eighteen years old. In Shakespeare's play, he is naturally portrayed as a rather obnoxious character, and it is easy for Henry V to be made to look heroic by comparison. Contrary to his major part in the play, the real Dauphin was not present at the Battle of Agincourt at all, but the self-centred speeches Shakespeare puts into his mouth do reflect an attitude often associated with the French in this encounter.

John the Fearless, Duke of Burgundy, who would have been the obvious choice to take overall control of the French army, had absented himself, abiding by an agreement he had already made with the English. Moreover, the French leaders did not really want him there, fearing that his presence would result in another quarrel with the supporters of the Orléans faction. Another absentee was John, Duke of Brittany, the son of Henry's stepmother Joanna of Navarre; the duke had deliberately set off both late and slowly so as to avoid arriving in time for the battle.

It was thus the younger members of the French aristocracy and royalty who wanted to take the battle to the English, assuming that numeric superiority would ensure their success. Charles d'Orléans (Duke Louis's son), Jean de Bourbon and Jean d'Alençon were among those who could not wait to make their names in battle. The older, more experienced military leaders tended to be less complacent; they could see the danger in giving battle, but they were overruled.

In truth, Henry V's reasons for pursuing the military campaign in France were more complex than a simple belief in the rightness of his cause. In fact, even ignoring Salic Law, his own claim on the throne was less good than those of some of his cousins. War was always popular with the English people, except when it led to higher taxation, and this was one of the times when the king needed popular opinion on his side. Henry saw the main chance, and pursued his alliance with the Burgundians, thus dividing the opposition. The French knew what he was planning, and showed their displeasure by refusing to pay the tribute that was due to him as a result of his grandfather's earlier victories.

The story about the Dauphin sending the tennis balls as a present to the playful prince does have some basis in fact, although it was probably a smaller quantity than Shakespeare suggests – but Shakespeare never missed an opportunity for a dramatic scene like the one where the treasure chest is opened and Henry responds with a suitable series of metaphors about playing a set that will defeat the French king and turning the tennis balls into 'gun-stones', meaning cannonballs. The tennis balls were, it is said, delivered to Henry at Kenilworth while he was occupied with the building of his new pleasure-palace, The Pleasance, making the gift an even more telling insult towards a young man who still enjoyed many of the same pursuits he had taken up prior to his accession.

In reality, propriety demanded that Henry made some attempt to negotiate a peaceful solution before asking parliament to fund an invasion, but his terms for giving up his claim on France were extravagant. He wanted all the territory his ancestors had lost. He wanted two million crowns in supposedly unpaid ransoms. In addition, he wanted to marry one of the French king's daughters, which would still have put him in with a chance of the throne if there was no surviving male heir. Not Isabelle, who had already died, but there were younger sisters available, notably the beautiful, blonde Catherine, who was not yet fourteen years old. On this occasion, the French said no.

On 16 April 1415, when he had already begun recruiting, the king held a great 'Council of War' in London. Knowing that he would be out of the country for some time, he appointed one of his brothers Regent of England. Not Thomas, whose military experience was too valuable for Henry to leave him behind, but John, Duke of Bedford, who proved a competent administrator. Their youngest brother, Humphrey, Duke of Gloucester, would accompany the king on campaign. Henry's target date for setting out for France was 1 July.

From Southampton to Harfleur

While collecting his forces, Henry stayed at various places in the south of England, including Wolvesey Castle in Winchester, a former bishop's palace next to the cathedral. It was there that he received an embassy from the French, a last-gasp attempt to avoid war. A year earlier, when three bishops, including Beaufort, had gone to France to negotiate on Henry's behalf, they had been promptly sent back, 'a laughing-stock', but the threat from England was suddenly more urgent and the French seemed prepared to talk.

Henry entertained them to dinner, heard Mass with them, and then listened to what Guillaume de Boisratier, Archbishop of Bourges, had to say. Boisratier carried letters of greeting from King Charles VI, reiterating previous offers. It was already July, and the negotiators hurried to try to reach an agreement on the question of a dowry for Catherine of Valois. Not long before, at Titchfield Abbey, Henry had thoroughly checked old documents to find out what he might be entitled to. Now he demanded not only the duchies of Anjou and Touraine, but everything else his ancestors had ever owned ('all that belonged to the first Edward', as Lydgate's poem put it). The English demands were so stringent that the French ambassadors knew their king would never accept them, and the negotiations were terminated.

Henry moved on from Wolvesey to Portchester Castle near Fareham, a comfortable royal residence that had been refurbished by Richard II only twenty years earlier. The castle would have put the new king in mind of his great-grandfather, King Edward III, who had stayed there just before setting out on the highly successful Crécy campaign. However, while resident there, Henry was obliged to deal with a conspiracy to depose him, which became known as the 'Southampton Plot'. The would-be rebels planned to replace him with Edmund Mortimer, Earl of March, the youth who had been Richard II's intended heir and whom Owain Glyndŵr had sought to abduct ten years earlier. The young earl, now aged about twenty-three, was already in the king's bad books because his marriage to Anne Stafford (yet another descendant of King Edward III) had taken place without Henry's approval. When approached by the conspirators, Mortimer chose not to risk further discord and reported them to the king. The ringleader was the earl's brother-in-law, Richard, Earl of Cambridge.

His two lieutenants, Lord Scrope and Sir Thomas Grey, were put on trial with Cambridge in Southampton. The Red Lion Inn claims to have been the venue for the trial, but is not quite old enough to be the same building.

Although there remains some doubt about Lord Scrope's true motivation, he was found guilty. Since Scrope was said to be a man 'whom the king had loved more than all others'[1] and reportedly often slept in the king's chamber, it would be surprising if Henry did not give him the benefit of any doubt, thus there is a question mark as to whether they really were that intimate. Scrope was executed along with the other two nobles, after being examined by a commission in which the Earl of March played an active role. Henry showed a certain amount of leniency when dealing with Cambridge's family, allowing his wife Maud to carry on as normal and his son to inherit not only the earldom but his uncle's titles. As Richard, Duke of York, Cambridge's son would go to be the nemesis of the next King of England.

The Earl of March, to counter any residual suspicion, received a formal pardon and was thereafter one of Henry's closest allies, fighting for him throughout his French campaigns. After Henry's death, however, he would fall out with the regents of Henry VI and would end his life as a prisoner in the insalubrious surroundings of Trim Castle in Ireland, the very same place where Henry V had been confined as a teenager.

But for now, twenty-eight-year-old Henry, only two years into his reign, gathered his army and the ships he had acquired and headed for Harfleur, an important and strategic port. It was the foremost port of north-western France, and would not be eclipsed by Le Havre until a hundred years later. There were other, smaller ports along that section of the coast, at l'Eure and Sainte-Adresse; these have also now been

---

1. Mayor of York's Register.

absorbed into Le Havre. At this point, it is worth mentioning Henry's role in the development of the royal navy. Inexperienced in fighting overseas as he was, he had nevertheless recognised that he would need a sea-going fleet if he was ever going to exert control over France. By 1410, when he was still Prince of Wales, he already owned two ships.

In the period of uneasy truce negotiated by Richard II between England and France, piracy in the surrounding seas had become increasingly normal. In the first two years of Henry's reign, he had succeeded in amassing over a thousand ships, of varying sizes and capability, in readiness for this expedition. Henry's personal flagship, the *Trinity Royal*, was built at Greenwich and was very large by contemporary standards, capable of carrying 200 men. William Catton, a long-time servant of the king, was appointed 'Keeper of the King's Ships' in 1413. The king must have been an occasional visitor at Greenwich, looking over the progress being made by the shipbuilders. The *Trinity Royal* now lay at anchor at Spithead, a sheltered area of the Solent off Portsmouth, and the king was finally ready to set sail on 11 August.

After a two-day voyage, the English force landed at Frileuse, a small settlement at the mouth of the River Seine, in glorious weather. Sir John Fastolf – a loyal follower who, along with Sir John Oldcastle, is believed to have been a model for Shakespeare's Falstaff – later claimed that he had been the first man off the ship and wading ashore. Certainly, Henry later gifted him the Manoir de Frileuse in recognition of his service. The Manoir de Vitarval, now in the Le Havre suburb of Sainte-Adresse, stands on the site previously occupied by a castle which the English later garrisoned, but is a much newer building. Sainte-Adresse has been suggested as a possible alternative landing place for at least part of the fleet.

The king himself sought a suitable place to take up residence for the duration, and made for the Priory of Graville, located on high ground overlooking the mouth of the Seine. The abbey was seriously damaged during the Second World War, has been considerably restored since then, and is open to visitors, as are its gardens, a popular recreation area for locals. The 'Balade des escaliers côté ville', a walking route around Le Havre designed for tourists, using the city's many 'escaliers' or staircases, ends at the Escalier de l'Abbaye. The priory church of Graville still retains the Romanesque features that make it a notable example of Normandy's architectural history.

The French had no navy to speak of, and had anticipated an English attack via Boulogne, or possibly an approach via Bordeaux, the capital of English-held Aquitaine, previously used as a bridgehead by Edward III. The latter alternative would have meant negotiating the notoriously rough waters of the Bay of Biscay. Harfleur was, however, a long-term objective. The French had been using it as a base for shipping troops to Wales to assist Owain Glyndŵr and it was also the enemy's starting point for communications with the Scots (who in June had made a rather feeble attempt to invade the north of England). Taking it – and more importantly, keeping it – would cut the French off from their main northern ports and force them to use La Rochelle, much further south.

Despite the importance of Harfleur, there were only a hundred men guarding the port, and Henry expected to take it easily. He must have believed that the town's fortifications, hastily constructed earlier in the Hundred Years' War to fend off English attacks, were vulnerable. He micro-managed the siege, but it was not as simple as he had anticipated. The ramparts were impressive, and the walls sported no fewer than twenty-six towers. Mont Lecomte, where the priory and castle were situated, overlooked Harfleur to the west, and Mont Cabert stood on the town's eastern flank. The English had to get up onto the high ground in order to attack – Henry to the west, between the coast and the town, and his brother Thomas to the east. Peter Hoskins and Anne Curry have identified the junction of the present-day Rue de l'Eure and Rue des Remparts as the approximate position of the front line of Henry's besieging troops, and they believe that Thomas's position was in the vicinity of the present-day Rue du Calvaire.

The defending force began by flooding the land around the town walls; an indirect result was that dysentery spread rapidly among the besieging army, an early fatality from the disease being Bishop Courtenay, Henry's trusted adviser, in mid-September. Raoul de Gaucourt, a French hero of the Hundred Years' War, was now able to negotiate the salt marshes with the much-needed relief force of 300 men and make his way into the town. Henry spotted his error too late and took action to block the mouth of the River Lézarde, which ran through the middle of the town to join the Seine. Even after this setback, he was confident of a favourable end to the siege. His brother Thomas had succeeded in crossing the river and capturing a convoy carrying supplies to the other side of Harfleur.

The English mined the castle walls, to be met with counter-mines by the opposition under Gaucourt. Henry had learned how to use artillery while fighting in Wales, and this knowledge paid off. One of the guns he deployed at Harfleur was 'Messager', a successor to the cannon of the same name he had lost at Aberystwyth. According to Lydgate, it gave good service at Harfleur. Likewise, 'The King's Daughter' was a replacement for the one he had lost at Harlech. There are records of some of these larger guns being constructed at London and Bristol during 1414 and early 1415. It is said that the king 'gave himself no rest' until all the guns were set up in accordance with his specifications. Palisades of thick planks were constructed around the muzzles of the guns to make it harder for them to be targeted by the enemy's cross-fire.

Working closely with the king, his chief engineer Master Giles had devised a secret weapon for use in the bombardment. This contraption fired the equivalent of an incendiary shell against the wooden sections of the barbican, and it worked extremely well, quickly setting the gateway on fire. The English were able to take the barbican, but not to enter the town. Although they had succeeded in breaching the walls – hence the famous speech in Shakespeare's play: 'Once more unto the breach, etc' – it was actually another five days before the town surrendered. The conventions of warfare allowed the besieged to be given a few days' grace to meet a deadline for surrendering if it was thought that the siege might be relieved. Not until 30 August did the French even begin to raise an army, and by mid-September, the Dauphin still did not have enough men to relieve Harfleur. The citizens had anticipated the arrival of a relief force but eventually gave up hope when they realised it was not going to appear.

*****

The siege had taken four weeks in all, during which time Henry did not allow any of his men to return home, however sick they might be. Raoul de Gaucourt gave himself up, on a promise from Henry to allow the French prisoners to ransom themselves after Agincourt, but Henry was unforgiving. When the time came, he added further impossible conditions, with the result that de Gaucourt spent several years in prison and would not be released until after Henry's death.

Henry was determined to make his presence felt in France, and emphasised his claim on the throne by sitting in state at the top of a slope on nearby Mont Lecomte to receive the surrender of Harfleur. The leading citizens were made to approach him with ropes around their necks in a traditional gesture of subjugation, just as the famous 'Burghers of Calais' had done in the presence of his great-grandfather, King Edward III. Above Henry's head was a golden canopy, and alongside him was his crowned helmet. Le Havre's 'Parc de la Ferme de Mont Lecomte' can be visited on foot, entering via the present-day Rue Edouard Vaillant. This five-hectare green space, now a public park, overlooks Harfleur. The trees now seen when looking down at the town were planted only in later centuries, so Henry would have had a clear view from this spot.

Henry had no intention of taking physical revenge on the representatives of the town of Harfleur, and instead gave them a good supper. Remaining conscious of the need to humble himself before

God, to whom he ascribed the victory, the king next day descended on foot into the town, and walked barefoot to the church of St Martin to pray. The townspeople were removed from their homes within days and sent to Rouen in the care of Marshal Boucicaut (whom we shall meet again later). From now on, it was Henry's intention that Harfleur would be occupied by loyal Englishmen and women.

The bell tower of St Martin's is separate from the church, and had been almost destroyed by the English artillery, but it would be rebuilt. For almost two decades, Harfleur would remain in English hands, though nowadays St Martin's Church is a living memorial to its liberation in 1435, when the bell tolled 104 times to mark the end of the English occupation, each toll representing one of the 104 heroic residents who helped to free the town. The tolling of the bell on the anniversary of this event took place every year for a couple of centuries afterwards. Following the damage done to the church by the siege itself, it was almost completely reconstructed a hundred years later, and would again be badly damaged during the First World War. A new set of stained-glass windows was installed during the 2010s.

A bronze statue of Jean de Grouchy, dating from 1875, has pride of place in the town. Grouchy may have fought on the French side at Agincourt, but is best remembered as the town's 'liberator', having led the French rebels in 1435, at the age of eighty-one! Although his efforts to drive out the English were successful, Grouchy himself was killed in the attempt.

Today, Harfleur has been reduced to the status of a suburb of Le Havre, but it retains some of its medieval buildings and portions of the ramparts that would have been relatively new in Henry's time. The town is no longer a seaport, and is connected to the Seine only by the Canal de Tancarville, constructed in 1887. Archaeological excavations have revealed the route of the medieval city walls; surviving sections that can be seen include the Porte de Rouen, one of the town's three original gates. Built in the 1390s, it has been partly restored, showing off the artillery platform built by the English after Henry left for Agincourt.

The Priory Museum, located in a former medieval inn called the Hotel des Portuguais, contains finds covering a long period of the town's history. Further work is planned to highlight more of Harfleur's archaeological heritage. Other buildings dating to the fifteenth century include the Hôtel Braquehaye and the Hôtel de la Rose Blanche, now a library.

*****

After a couple of weeks in France, the king had written home to say that the siege was nearly over and, after that, he would be marching on Paris. This may not have been his true intention; it may have been propaganda or an attempt to throw the French off the scent. It had taken the English over a month to complete their capture of Harfleur, and they were running short of time. The weather had been very hot, which exacerbated the outbreak of dysentery; many of Henry's men had died and those who were too sick to fight had to be sent home, in the care of Henry's brother Thomas. It was also necessary to leave some men behind to garrison Harfleur. Thus Henry had lost over 2,000 men before he even launched the hardest part of his expedition.

He had also left behind his uncle, Thomas Beaufort, Earl of Dorset, an able commander. Putting Beaufort in charge of Harfleur as its 'Captain' would turn out to be a sensible move, since in the years that followed considerable pressure was put on the garrison by their French neighbours. It sometimes proved difficult to obtain supplies and there would be occasions when Dorset, remote from any hope of assistance from England, was forced into armed confrontation, notably the Battle of Valmont in the following year, where his troops would be lucky to escape a hiding. The Captain's residence may have been at the building now called the Hôtel de la Rose Blanche, where medieval architectural features are still visible.

The departure from Harfleur marked the point where Henry's problems really started. The king did not have nearly enough men to march on Paris as had been proposed, and he was effectively on the run. The French had temporarily settled their internal quarrels and were now amassing a sizeable army, but there seemed a good chance the English would outrun them and reach Calais without any further setbacks. Henry had intended to make his way along the northern coast of France, but the French leaders foresaw this and by now they were ready - or almost ready – to meet him in battle.

Why Calais, when Henry was already close to a major port? Was it because he wanted to return home from a bigger port, one that was in English hands and where he might have been able to stay and await reinforcements, or was marching across northern France a way of taunting the enemy? Or was it because returning via Harfleur would be seen as a failure of the expedition, even though the port had been taken? Henry's ships had gone home – there was nothing much now in port at Harfleur that would enable him to transport his remaining forces back to England. If he marched on, the French army would follow him rather than attacking Harfleur, giving Dorset the time he needed to make England's latest gains secure.

Another factor that may have played a part in the decision is that the marshy area around Harfleur was now rife with disease. Getting his remaining troops away from that unhealthy atmosphere might have made the march to Calais an attractive proposition, given that the French were having difficulty getting their act together. The king himself wrote that he was leaving Harfleur because of 'the grievous pestilence that was prevalent'. Perhaps he had some idea that reducing the overcrowding would improve conditions for the garrison he was leaving behind, as well as for the men he was taking with him.

It has been suggested that the English were interested in establishing a 'pale' at Harfleur, comparable to the Pale of Calais, a buffer area of about twenty square miles around the port, acquired by Edward III in a treaty with the French. The Pale had proved very handy as an outpost on the continent, but the limited manpower available to Henry made the prospect of doing the same at Harfleur a non-starter. Moreover, Harfleur had been badly damaged in the course of the siege, and rebuilding the defences was going to take time. The town did not have the infrastructure to support Henry's troops for long.

Henry V seems to have been a man who made many mistakes but was good at learning from them, and his later campaigns in France illustrate the lessons he had learned from the Agincourt campaign. As he left Harfleur, he would be passing through lands that he believed were rightly his. He must have known that he would not be welcomed by the people of France, even in his ancestral stronghold of Normandy, but he was careful to insist that he was in his own country and to exert as much control as possible over the activities of his soldiers. There was to be no stealing or arson, he declared, as the French were his subjects. If he was expecting gratitude, he was much mistaken.

It may seem odd to us that Henry should even have needed to make such a command, but the troops were travelling through unfamiliar country without enough provisions for such a long march, and were obliged to forage for food. Anything that might slow them down had to be left behind in Harfleur, including the cannon (thus we can be certain that there were no plans for a pitched battle). Many men would have been separated by some distance from the main party of cavalry and baggage which travelled on the major roads, such as they were. During the march, at least one soldier was hanged for stealing from a church. On several occasions before meeting the French army, the English were subject to attacks from small groups of locals who may have hoped to pick off stray individuals but were generally subdued without much difficulty.

It was never Henry's intention to occupy any of the walled towns en route to Calais. Any protection they might have offered his men was more than outweighed by the risk of loss of English lives, every one of which was now a valuable asset. Once inside, the town's defences might have become a trap, leading to the English themselves coming under siege. Moreover, since Henry was not planning to meet the French in battle, avoiding densely populated areas would have made it more difficult for his enemies to track his position, giving him every hope of reaching Calais before a French army could reach him.

A few miles north of Harfleur lies the town of Montivilliers, connected to Harfleur by road via another of the town gates, the Porte de Montivilliers, which no longer stands. Parts of the town walls do survive, including the remains of a tower, the Tour Vatellière. Montivilliers' defences would have made it a daunting prospect to a potential attacker, even to an army that was fully equipped with artillery. The English gave it a wide berth, avoiding any serious trouble with the locals. The abbey, located in Place François Mitterrand, was home to about thirty nuns, who later evacuated and moved to Rouen, fearing a return visit.

Similarly, there was only a minor skirmish at the next town, Fécamp. The English would return there four years later and the next time they would not hesitate. From here, Henry's men covered the distance to Dieppe in good time, and planned to cross the Somme at Blanchetaque near Abbeville, the very same spot where his ancestor, Edward III, had defeated a French force in 1346. They moved a little way inland towards Arques, where there was a bridge over the River Béthune. Now known as Arques-la-Bataille (in recognition of a battle that took place there more than 150 years later), it still boasts some fine castle remains, but the castle Henry saw was a much smaller eleventh-century affair. Here the garrison at first fired on the English, but they were able to negotiate a passage unhindered.

The army progressed to the city of Eu, outside which there was yet another skirmish. They succeeded in crossing the River Bresle in the Beauchamps/Incheville area. The castle of Eu, the place where William the Conqueror had married Matilda of Flanders in the mid-eleventh century, is no longer standing, and has been replaced by a sixteenth-century chateau with a museum dedicated to Louis-Philippe (1773-1850), the last king of France. However, the medieval church of Notre-Dame et Saint Laurent survives. The nearby village of Incheville retains a number of medieval buildings that would have existed and possibly been seen by Henry V, including the Church of Saint-Lubin, and the suburb of Gousseauville has an oratory dedicated to Saint-Léger; the twenty-first century finds the latter in very poor condition.

Having received a warning that the nearest ford over the River Somme was blocked by the enemy and that the French were waiting for him on the opposite bank, Henry realised that the reinforcements he had expected from Calais would not be able to get through, and was forced to change his plans. At Corbie, where the Somme makes a loop, Henry hoped to take a shortcut across the ford, but he was met with local resistance on 17 October, and this time his opponents were too numerous to be disregarded.

Corbie's seventy-year-old walls included eighteen defensive towers and it was too daunting a prospect for the English even to consider making an assault. The town still boasts the disused medieval church of Saint Etienne – not to be confused with its grander neighbour, the Abbey Church of Saint Pierre de Corbie, the only survivor of the Benedictine monastery around which the town grew up; the English king would have been interested to hear of its great library and scriptorium. Of greater relevance for us are the ruins of a watchtower, part of the original town walls, preserved within the grounds of a local school.

The encounter between the town's garrison and Henry's army probably took place to the south, well outside the town walls. The English battle standard was temporarily lost to the raiding party, but they soon rallied and drove off their attackers. The family of John Bromley of Baddington in Cheshire, a poor relation of Lord Bourchier, still believe that Bromley was the man who recovered the standard and that he was rewarded with a pension for doing so.

Prisoners taken during the skirmish revealed that the French were already amassing an enormous army at Péronne, only about twenty miles away. Péronne, though it was not on Henry's route on this occasion, also contains some medieval survivals. Its castle, originally constructed by King Philip II of France, was restored after the First World War and now houses a museum, the 'Historial de la Grande Guerre'. The interesting Gothic church of Saint-Jean-Baptiste de Péronne, which somehow survived wartime bombing, was not built in its present form until the sixteenth century; in 1415, all that would have been seen was a modest medieval chapel.

Henry is said to have spent the night in the village of Caix. Next day there was another setback, when the town of Nesle offered resistance. They too knew that the French army was close enough to come to their aid if necessary, and they were well-defended by walls strengthened with eight towers and ditches on all sides, kept full by a small river. There were also several outlying forts in the vicinity, none of which survive except in place names such as le Chateau Fort. Accordingly, Nesle refused to do the usual deal – food in return for a promise not to attack. Henry's wrath was unleashed on the surrounding villages, which he burned to the ground despite his earlier declarations of good intent towards the citizens of the region.

The modern town of Nesle retains little of its medieval charm, though the line of the ramparts is marked by the ditches that ring the settlement to the north. The Château Boisset, now long gone, stood alongside the present-day D2930; a few remains are still visible. The town's medieval church, on the site of its successor, was destroyed along with Château Boisset in 1918.

As they marched inland, further away from any French scouts, the English finally managed to locate a ford in the Béthencourt/Voyennes area. The lands around the river in this spot were prone to flooding and it was later canalised. While trying to find a place to cross, some of Henry's men may have found themselves entering the villages of Mareuil-Caubert and Eaucourt-sur-Somme. The people of the latter had demolished their castle many decades before in order to avoid it being captured and used as a base by English invaders. It would be rebuilt in the 1430s, but would soon be fought over again and is now a complete ruin.

By nightfall on 19 October, Henry and his army were on the northern bank of the Somme, slipping past French troops led by Marshal Boucicaut. After doing so, they rested near Athies, where fragmentary remains of medieval walls can still be seen. Athies, like Nesle, had been snatched from the Armagnacs by John the Fearless ten years earlier; its inhabitants had not put up a fight on that occasion, and chose not to do so now. The surviving church was substantially rebuilt after the First World War, but does have some medieval sections. The castle, however, was demolished in the eighteenth century. Other members of the host may have camped at Monchy-Lagache, where they would have admired the church of St Pierre. The Germans occupied the village during the First World War, and, as at Athies, the structure that is to be seen now was almost completely rebuilt afterwards.

Though buoyed up by their success in crossing the River Somme, the English must have been exhausted. The journey had proved considerably longer than anticipated, and it is unlikely that many of the ordinary soldiers had their own horses. Having mustered their troops and overtaken him on the way to Calais, the French had blocked Henry's way home and ensured that any reinforcements never reached him. Crossing the Somme had added an extra hundred miles to his journey, the route eventually leading the English further and further inland, ever closer to danger. The map shows the detours they were forced to make. It should not be forgotten that maps at this period of history were neither easily obtainable nor accurate, which was one of the reasons that Henry wanted to keep close to the coast. There seems little doubt that he lost his bearings once or twice en route. This is one of the reasons why, whether we try to follow in his footsteps either on foot or by vehicle, we can rarely be entirely sure that we are on the right road.

As they came closer to their planned destination, the English were confronted by French heralds, who demanded their surrender in vain. It was clear that Henry felt he had gone too far to give up, and he was not prepared to lose face by accepting their terms. It is possible that the French issued a challenge to meet them in pitched battle, something for which the English were inadequately prepared; it seems that Henry and his knights got kitted out in their armour, just in case. If the French were going to attack, Henry expected them to do so from the direction of Péronne, but he skirted the city with little incident. Soon his men were passing through places whose names have become familiar to us because they were part of the Western Front during the First World War of 1914-1918 – Albert, Fricourt and Mametz.

Albert (known as Ancre until the seventeenth century), despite the reputation for indestructibility of the 'Golden Virgin' on top of its church tower, was almost completely flattened during the war years. Notre-Dame de Brebières, the medieval statue from which the church took its name, does however survive and has been magnificently restored; its age is uncertain. Like Albert, Fricourt and Mametz are nowadays more notable for their wartime remains, especially the many cemeteries administered by the Commonwealth War Graves Commission. These are a timely reminder of the extent to which this region has been fought over during past centuries.

The town was well-fortified and Henry's army avoided it, passing through Miraumont and thence to Louvencourt, Acheux-en-Amiénois and Forceville, smaller settlements where overnight resting-places could be found. Some of this may have been in underground passages, reputedly constructed by early Christians but no longer accessible. Ironically, the Château de l'Épine at Acheux, which incorporates two of the towers of the later medieval castle, is now a hotel. Almost all the buildings in this area post-date the fifteenth century.

The River Authie remained to be crossed, and this was no simple task. The crossing near Thièvres required the army to make a steep descent before an equally steep slope on the other side. Some of Henry's forces may have crossed further north, closer to the major town of Doullens. The king is believed to have spent the night at Bonnières on the River Canche, whilst the Duke of York advanced as far as Frévent, only to find that the French had broken the bridge in an attempt to stop the English crossing the river. With Henry absent, York may have lost control, since it is alleged that some of his men plundered the nearby Cistercian abbey of Cercamp. The abbey was finally destroyed in the nineteenth century, and replaced with a grander edifice that opened to visitors in 2012.

Now, a couple of days after the encounter with the heralds, the English were able to look down from a ridge and view the extent of the French army, a sight that must have put the fear of God into Henry as well as most of his men. There was yet another river to cross, the Ternoise, smaller than the Canche but still necessitating a steep descent followed by a steep climb. They crossed at the village of Blangy, still armoured and prepared for battle, but encountered little opposition. So, on the evening of 24 October 1415, finding their way to Calais again blocked by the French, they encamped, exhausted, at Maisoncelle and Henry made up his mind to give battle the following day. It is said that he ordered total silence to be kept in the camp overnight, in order that the men could get some rest before an encounter he knew might be the destruction of them all. Their quietness caused some of the French to believe that the English had run away during the night. The French army, meanwhile, was making a considerable racket. The French chronicler Monstrelet, however, claims it was the other way round: that the French army was quiet, whilst the English played loud music.

English history tends to keep quiet about the fact that Henry now tried to make a deal with the French, and sent out negotiators to the enemy camp, even offering to give up Harfleur if they would let him pass. They refused, confident in the knowledge that they had a large enough force to outnumber him and fully aware of the state his army was in. They had even chosen the battlefield. Yet instead of attacking straight away, they had waited. They were expecting more men, just to be on the safe side. It was not until late on the morning of the 25th that they were ready for battle, thus giving Henry time to make a battle plan and use the terrain to his advantage, finding a relatively narrow place where his army was protected by woods on each side. It did not escape his notice that the field had been recently ploughed, and he gained a further advantage by stopping on the firm ground so that the French had to advance over the boggy ground to reach him.

On the morning of the battle, the king appeared in his full splendour, dressed so as to appeal to the national pride of his army and bolster their morale. He wore a complete suit of plate armour, a relatively new development among English knights which might have struck spectators as 'high-tech'. As king, his father had abandoned the arms of King Richard II, and over his armour Henry wore a surcoat decorated with the lions of England and the fleur-de-lis of France, somewhat in imitation of the royal arms of his opposite number, King Charles VI. His helmet was ornamented with a crown, an undoubted fact too often dismissed as a myth by modern writers. Thus clad, he heard three masses before mounting his horse in readiness for battle. It is known that he made an encouraging speech to those within earshot, but no one can be sure exactly what he said.

It has been suggested that Henry V was not as popular with the English as Charles VI (nicknamed 'le Bien-Aimé') was with the French, simply because his father was a usurper and Henry himself a latecomer to the throne. This suggestion fails to take into account a number of factors. Henry had not been king for long, but the English people, particularly the soldiers, had grown used to him through the years of fighting in Wales as well as his early involvement in the government of the realm. His father may have been unpopular, but the younger Henry benefited from his youthful and glamorous image in much the same way as the grandsons of Queen Elizabeth II have done in the twenty-first century. Moreover, the king had three handsome younger brothers who had proved themselves in battle and/or government. Most importantly, the French king and his sons were not present on the battlefield, but the English king was, and this was critical to the morale of the troops. Had Henry died in action that day, his brother Humphrey would no doubt have replaced him as a rallying point.

According to tradition, there was a castle near the spot Henry had chosen to make his stand. Only after his victory did Henry discover its name, by asking the French herald Montjoie, who told him it was Azincourt. This later became corrupted into 'Agincourt' in the English language, becoming the name of the most famous battle ever fought by an English king. The present-day village of Azincourt did not exist at the time, and there remains some doubt about the exact location of the battlefield although, as with Shrewsbury, there is little evidence to suggest that it did not take place exactly where tradition says that it did.

Henry's Army

Much attention has been given to dispelling the 'myth' of the Welsh bowmen, but the truth is that the border was somewhat flexible, and it is not always easy to identify men who had left Wales for England to avoid the consequences of their previous service to Henry's enemies. Acquiring fighting men required a kind of contract, called an 'indenture of war', with those of his subjects whom he asked to supply troops. It specified how many men, with what skills, were to be supplied, and how much they were to be paid. Some of the original documents drawn up for the Agincourt campaign survive in the National Archives. A total of 290 such contracts are known to have been agreed, some for just a handful of men, others for many more.

Around 400 of the archers at Agincourt are thought to have been Welsh, out of a total of about 4,000 archers, but many came from the border regions. Nobody knows exactly what the total population of England, or Wales, was in 1415, and the estimates vary wildly. What is certain is that Owain Glyndŵr's rebellion had been in full flow less than ten years before the French campaign, and those responsible for recruiting the army would have made a very careful selection when considering men from the principality.

There were two types of archer: household archers and regular yeoman archers. Household archers tended to have better equipment. But the effective use of the longbow required immense skill and strength, so young men in some regions, including South Wales, trained for years to achieve this. This was in contrast to the use of the crossbow, which the French favoured because it called for very little training. So most of the archers were, up to a point, professional soldiers. By all accounts, the adult Henry was skilled in archery, so he knew what he was about when he was deciding how best to make use of them.

Archers would continue to be a major portion of the fighting force for many years to come. Local sheriffs were instructed to take six wing feathers from every goose in their district for the purpose of flighting the arrows, and normally every archer would come equipped with a sheaf of at least forty arrows for use in battle. At close quarters, however, their bows and arrows were no use. When it came to that kind of fighting, they naturally did not rely on their longbows but ditched them and used all kinds of other weapons, often homemade, such as hatchets and clubs as well as knives. They wore no armour, because they needed freedom of movement. By the time they got to Agincourt after the long march from Harfleur, some had no shoes.

A man-at-arms in the Middle Ages looked something like Robocop, and was very difficult to kill when he was wearing armour. But, just like Robocop, such soldiers were ungainly, especially once they were off their horses. If they fell over, they could not get up without assistance. If they remained on the ground, there was a danger of them being trampled and/or suffocated, and this was what happened to many of the knights at Agincourt. Knights at this time were tending to use two-handed swords, but lances and various forms of mace or club and dagger might be used as well. Knights wore their arms on their surcoat and shield, but at Agincourt, King Henry was the only one who wore the royal coat-of-arms, and the crown on his helmet would have made him both a target and a rallying point. He did not have the luxury of using lookalikes as his father had been able to do at Shrewsbury.

On the French side, so many armoured knights had turned up, enthused at the idea of a chance to show the English who was boss after the loss of Harfleur, that they were given priority over the archers, who were strangely positioned in such a way that they could not make the maximum impact on the hostilities in the way the English and Welsh archers would. As with so many medieval battles, no one has yet come up with an incontrovertible description of how the two armies arranged themselves on the battlefield. No one really knows what the anonymous chaplain's eye-witness account (in Latin) means when it refers to the English archers being formed up in "wedges', and drawings can merely give an impression of how the armies *might* have looked before battle began.

There is no agreement on the numbers of men participating in the battle. The English army has been estimated at a minimum of 6,000 and a maximum of 10,000, whilst the size of the French army has been estimated at somewhere between 12,000 and 36,000. The ratio between the two sides is not likely to be lower than 4:3, nor would it have been higher than 6:1, which most historians these days think is probably a gross exaggeration, intended to make the victory seem even more remarkable than it was. At the same time, it has been said that the French deliberately exaggerated the number of men in the English army so as to make their defeat appear less shameful. We know for certain that Henry lost a lot of his men between the taking of Harfleur and his arrival at Azincourt, possibly as much as a quarter of his whole army. There is no doubt that the French were in the majority, but the exact ratio can never be known.

For much the same reason, doubt has been cast on the number of casualties on either side. In Shakespeare's famous final scenes,

Henry reads out the names of those who have been killed on the English side and concludes that only twenty-nine men in total have been lost. Conversely, some historians have argued that the total number of the French dead was actually in the hundreds rather than the thousands.

Whilst Henry would have preferred not to fight against such disadvantageous odds, his fear of the situation may not have been as great as we imagine. He had witnessed, or knew of, many battles in which skill and discipline had overcome brute strength. Importantly, he also believed that God was on his side.

The Battle

The French had held off their attack, even though they already outnumbered the English, and anticipated that the English would desert in large numbers when attacked. They lined up in three rows, where the English had only one, which took up the whole of the space between the two woods, with Henry in the middle and the Duke of York on one side. The elderly Lord Camoys (the second husband of Harry Hotspur's widow) was on the left, and the archers were under the command of another veteran, Sir Thomas Erpingham. Bearing in mind that the space available for fighting was very narrow, this meant that the French could not even deploy all their troops; many never got anywhere near the action. Whether cannon were ever deployed is uncertain; if so, they played no significant part in the battle.

Henry's strategy was to goad the French into attacking, so he moved his army forward. Those stakes they planted in the ground to protect the archers were not a myth or an invention of Shakespeare's. It was a relatively new tactic, but had been used successfully during the skirmish at Corbie to fend off the local cavalry. The stakes had to be pulled out and pushed back in after the archers moved forward, which was a big risk. To hammer the stakes into the ground, many of the archers would have used something called a warhammer, a versatile tool that doubled as an offensive weapon, with the pointed end being capable of killing even an armoured opponent on foot.

Shortly after moving forward, they fired their first volley of arrows, which was not returned by the French archers, who had been deployed in a rather awkward position, to the side of what we might call the infantry. Henry's archers were fully aware that their arrows were unlikely to penetrate the plate armour worn by the French knights, and, where the French were mounted, they aimed for the horses rather than their riders, which goes a long way towards explaining the outcome of the battle. The French charged, and the narrowness of the field resulted in a mudbath where many of the French, both on foot and on horseback, effectively drowned or were smothered. The defensive stakes certainly played a part in this success, but it would not be true to say that the French never reached the English front line.

The French knights could see that the ground was muddy, so they were nervous about charging on horseback. They could also see that the archers were going to be a force to be reckoned with, so they did not dare remove any of their armour. Thus many of the French attacked on foot, in all that heavy armour, and soon ended up in just as difficult a position as their horses would have been, floundering in the mud. It seems as though the very act of charging in heavy armour was quite exhausting, and the hail of arrows could be likened to an artillery bombardment in later wars, as it wore them down so that, by the time the English and the French were engaged in hand-to-hand combat, the English were much fresher and this gave them an advantage.

The contemporary accounts say that Henry himself was fully involved in this hand-to-hand fighting - the melée as it was known. The Duke of York, Edward of Norwich, a generation older than the king, was one of the few notable fatalities on the English side, and he probably met the same fate as many of the French knights, being suffocated in the mud. Some accounts suggest that Henry's younger brother Humphrey was almost a casualty too, and that the king saved him from serious injury or death by standing over him and fighting off the opposition single-handed. This sounds awfully like propaganda.

Many readers will have heard the myth that the V-sign originated from the English and Welsh archers holding up their two bow fingers to the French to show that they were still functioning. This is dependent on the truth of the popular story that the French had threatened, if they caught any of them, to cut off those two fingers, which were essential for operating a longbow. A contemporary French chronicler wrote that the English at Agincourt told their men that the French had threatened to cut off their first *three* fingers, all three of which would have been needed to draw a longbow. If such a threat was made, it was not genuine; the French would hardly have bothered when they could simply kill any archers that they caught. The French chronicler, Wavrin, says nothing about the English and Welsh archers holding up their fingers as a taunt, and in any case this explanation for how the V-sign originated has been current for less than fifty years.

Marshal Boucicaut commanded the first rank of the French army, whose charge was a disorganised one. Charles d'Albret, the Constable of France, who commanded the third rank of the French army, was an experienced soldier, who recognised the importance of taking advantage of his superior numbers. He tried to hold back the rest of the army from pushing forward, hoping to give the English time to wear themselves out before making a move, but he lost control after that first volley of arrows, as the mounted cavalry tried to push in front of the men-at-arms. As the space available grew narrower the further forward they went, the more they became squashed together and the result was not dissimilar to the Hillsborough football stadium disaster of 1989. After about half an hour, the first two ranks of the French army had thrown themselves on the English without doing any damage, and had been effectively defeated.

The third rank was now ready to attack, but in the meantime a French force, led by the Lord of Azincourt, had attacked the English from the rear, seizing the baggage train and killing the small force guarding it, which probably included some boy-soldiers. It is possible that this action was not approved by the French military leaders, since it was considered rather beneath the belt, an affront to chivalry. Not only that, but apparently one of the treasures stolen from the baggage was the king's spare crown! An unidentified chaplain (possibly, but probably not, Thomas Elmham), accommodated within the baggage train, escaped with his life and is thought to have been responsible for the *Gesta Henrici Quinti*, written from personal experience.

Henry's response was to begin killing the French prisoners, who by now almost outnumbered the English army and might have overpowered their guards if left alive. By doing so, Henry also reduced the likelihood of further French attacks. One of those who died was Antoine, Duke of Brabant, who had arrived late at the battle and may have been one of the prime movers in the attack on the baggage train. As a younger brother of John the Fearless, Antoine might reasonably have expected his life to be spared, since it had both a monetary and a diplomatic value. Many of the English were not too keen to obey the order to kill the prisoners, as it prevented them from demanding a ransom, and there is no record of what proportion of them were actually killed. Nevertheless, the action besmirched Henry's hitherto good reputation.

D'Albret, the Constable, was killed during the final French counter-attack. The veteran commander had not even wanted to fight, but would have been prepared to allow Henry's army passage to Calais because he was experienced enough to recognise the risks involved in giving battle. From beginning to end, the battle had taken only about three hours.

Many people still believe that the Battle of Agincourt was a highly significant victory for the English. British tourists visiting the village of Azincourt today are often disappointed to find no visible traces of the battlefield. Even the modern museum, opened in 2019 by Brigitte Macron, fails to meet their expectations. It is common for them to come away with the impression that the French are not interested in the battle simply because they lost. The truth is that, though Agincourt was a remarkable event that did have *some* significance at the time, it was by no means decisive. At best, it was a stepping stone in Henry's progress towards the domination of France.

In the initial aftermath of the battle, there was plenty of glory to be had. An estimated 9,000 Frenchmen had been killed, at least a hundred of them members of the aristocracy – 'a royal fellowship of death', as Shakespeare puts it. By contrast, the English had lost a maximum of about 2,000 men, few of whom were of high status. Many of their names are known, but most of their bodies were burned, or boiled, and the flesh removed from their bones so that these could be more easily returned home for burial.

Up to two thousand prisoners were taken, some of them important names such as Charles d'Orléans, a close relation of the French king and the second husband of the late Isabelle of Valois. Charles spent the next twenty-four years in England, and his fame rests mainly on the poetry he wrote while waiting to be ransomed. Another prisoner was Marshal Boucicaut, whose living form had been dug out from under a pile of dead French bodies; his luck did not hold out and he died six years later, still a prisoner in England. A prisoner who fared better was Arthur de Richemont, a future duke of Brittany and the son of Joanna of Navarre, the widow of Henry IV. Relations with the Bretons had been good, but Arthur was a close friend of the Dauphin Louis and was dedicated to the French cause against England. He remained a prisoner until 1420, when he would prove diplomatically useful to Henry V.

*****

One might have anticipated that the days immediately after the battle would be spent in celebration or perhaps in negotiation, but this was not the case. The English immediately resumed their journey towards

Calais, where they arrived four days later. The distance was short – less than fifty miles – but they were encumbered by the piles of battlefield plunder and the hordes of slow-moving prisoners. They would have been obliged to cross three small rivers – the Aa, the Bléquin and the Hem – before arriving at Guisnes, a city that had been taken by Edward III and fell within the Pale of Calais.

Henry may briefly have considered alternative courses of action, such as taking advantage of the carnage within the French army to march on Paris. However, with the limited resources at his disposal, he decided not to take any more chances. He returned to England within a few weeks, relying on the resumption of squabbles among the leading French factions to prevent his enemies from retaliating swiftly. There was no immediate acceptance of his claim to the French throne. What Agincourt would achieve, however, was to make him the most popular king who had ever ruled, or ever would rule, England.

Henry may have spent the night after the battle (26 October 1415) at Fauquembergues. The locals would doubtless already have heard that their lord had been killed at Azincourt and would not have wanted any trouble with the English. The town's thirteenth-century church, Saint-Léger, has survived, but the castle that dominated it has not. The high ground between the present-day Rue de Fruges and the cemetery is thought to have been its location. If Henry did stay here, there are no reminders of the occasion.

Two nights later, the army reached Guisnes. The Chateau de Guînes (as the town's name is now written), where Henry spent the night preparing for his triumphal entry into Calais, no longer exists, but the ancient motte, or mound, on which it stood, survives, topped with an eighteenth-century clock-tower, the Tour de l'Horloge. The tower has been converted into a small museum of living history that opened in 2002 and aims to tell the history of the city in a manner particularly appealing to younger visitors. The former castle had been captured by King Edward III in 1349, and remained in English hands,

Monnow Bridge, Monmouth, the only surviving fortified river bridge in Britain. (Photo by Philip Halling. License CC BY-SA 2.0, Wikimedia id=19338296)

Courtfield, Welsh_Bicknor, where Henry was cared for in childhood. (Photo by Stuart Wilding. License CC BY-SA 2.0, Wikimedia id=356747)

Richard II and Anne of Bohemia, from their tomb effigies. (Detail from an illustration in *History of England* (1905) by Samuel R. Gardiner)

Leicester Castle: former gateway. (Photo by Kris1973. License CC BY-SA 4.0, Wikimedia id=39823598)

Chester city walls. (Photo by Dave Craven. License CC BY-SA 3.0, Wikimedia id=28131357)

Former Wingfield's Tower, Shrewsbury. (Photo by David Dix. License CC BY-SA 2.0, Wikimedia id=75743537)

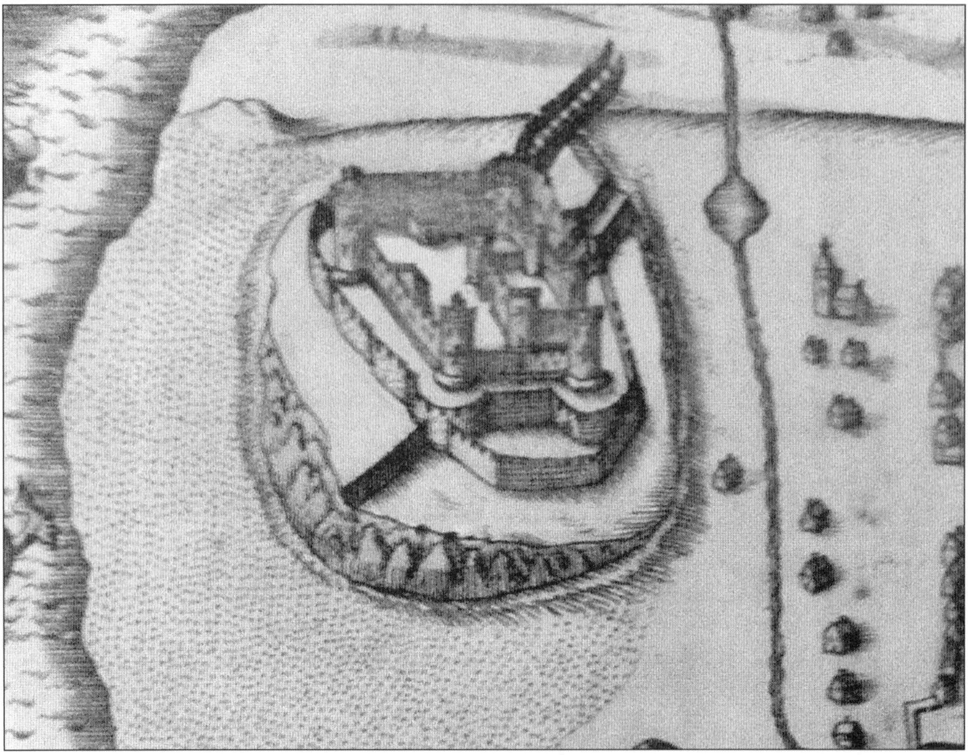

Plan of Harlech Castle, showing the proximity of the sea. (Detail from an illustration (1610) by John Speed)

Kenilworth Castle: remains of the Keep and John of Gaunt's Great Hall. (Photo by Robek. License CC BY 2.5. Wikimedia id=943392)

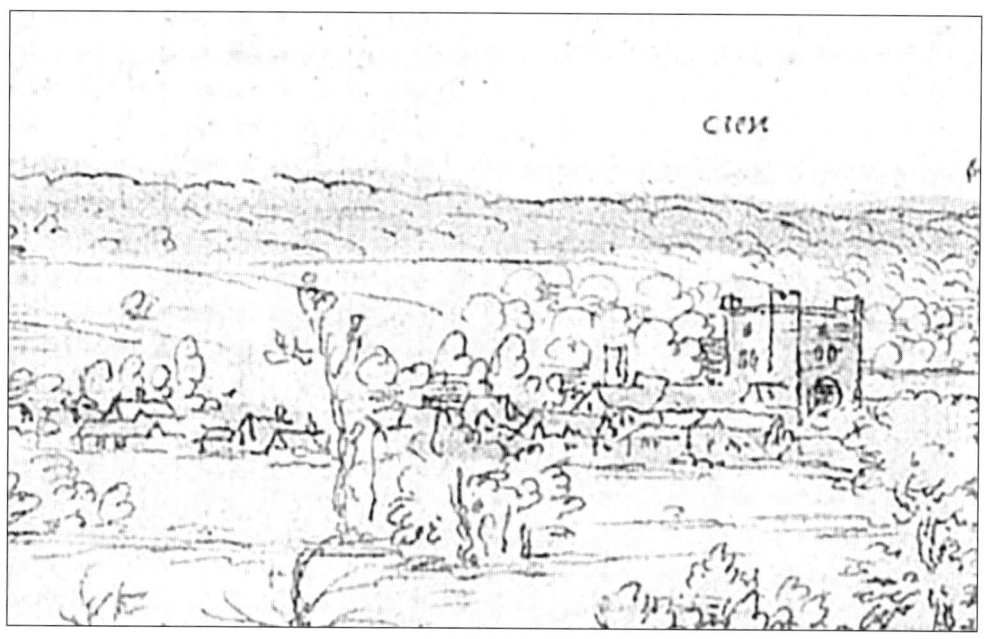

Above: Sheen Priory from the west. *(Detail from a sketch of Richmond Palace by Anton van den Wyngaerde (c. 1560))*

Right: The Corona Chapel, Canterbury Cathedral, once the site of Thomas Becket's shrine. (Photo by David Iliff. License CC BY-SA 3.0.)

The presumed battlefield of Agincourt. (Photo by Paul Hermans. License CC BY-SA 3.0, Wikimedia id=3190351)

Watchtower, Calais. (Photo by Lionel Allorge. License CC BY-SA 3.0, Wikimedia id=28268362)

Above: The medieval churches of Rouen (cathedral flanked by St Ouen and St Maclou). (Photo by Philippe Roudaut. License CC BY-SA 4.0, Wikimedia id=45385068)

Left: Siege of Rouen, showing the palisade built by Henry V. (Detail from an illustration in *A Short History of the English People* (1874) by J. R. Green)

Right: St Jean's Church, Troyes, where Henry and Catherine were married. (Photo by Superjuju10. License CC BY-SA 3.0, Wikimedia id=30419024)

Below: Catherine of Valois. (Detail from an illustration in the *Pageants of Richard Beauchamp* (c.1490))

Tour Jean-sans-Peur, Paris, as it may have looked in the 15th century. (Drawing by an unknown artist)

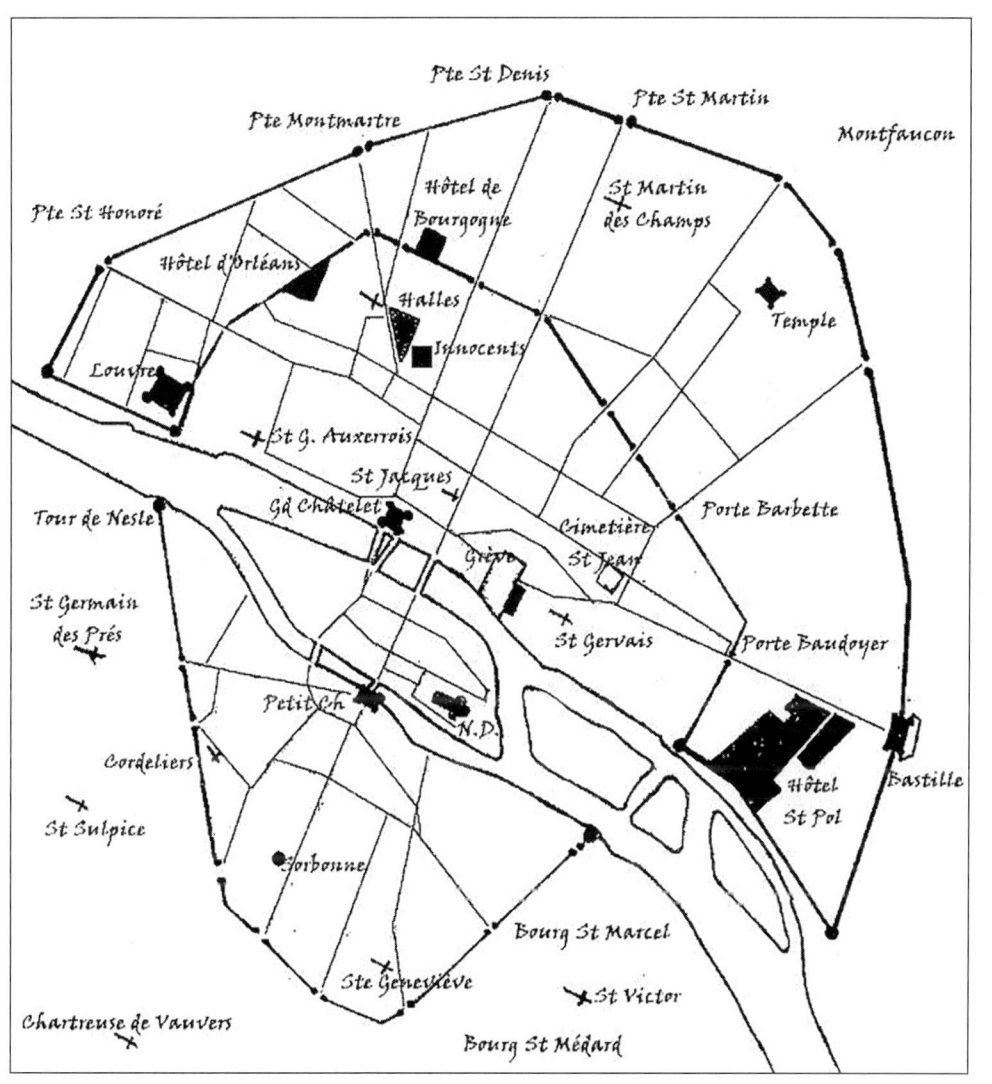

Plan of Paris in the 14th century. (Ville Lumière – Paris Ministries)

A surviving fragment of the city walls of Paris, built by Philip Augustus. (By CJ DUB. License CC BY-SA 3.0, Wikimedia id=7339300)

Statue of St Louis, Sainte Chapelle, Paris. (Photo by PHGCOM. License CC BY-SA 3.0, Wikimedia id=2663921)

Chateau de Vincennes, Keep. (Photo by Charly Bernard. License CC BY-SA 4.0, Wikimedia id=94748195)

but possession continued to be contested for another hundred years after the death of Henry V, eventually falling to the French along with Calais.

*****

If there is one French city that is familiar to British visitors, it is Calais. At the French end of what is traditionally the shortest route between France and the UK, it is where millions of British and French people have begun and ended their voyages across the English Channel, but its former status as a possession of the medieval monarchs of England is rarely thought of on these fleeting visits. The Tour du Guet, a thirteenth-century watchtower used for many centuries as a lighthouse, is one landmark that would have been a welcome sight to approaching Englishmen, particularly in the circumstances in which Henry's entourage now found themselves.

The Nieulay Bridge, across which Henry rode into Calais on 29 October 1415, spanned the River Hames, and was the main approach to the city. In fact, it was the only practicable way of entering from the land side, and was well defended. King Edward III had spent a year besieging the city before it fell back into English hands, and retaining it was considered vital, for commercial as well as sentimental reasons. Auguste Rodin's statue of the burghers of Calais outside the town hall, although only just over a hundred years old, represents the events of 1349 in a way designed to honour both the French and the English participants.

Few buildings in present-day Calais would have been known to Henry V. Even the citadel, the city's most prominent defensive structure, is a replacement for the medieval castle on whose site it was built in the sixteenth century. This was where Henry's great-uncle, Thomas of Woodstock, had been assassinated, possibly at the instigation of King Richard II, in 1398, while awaiting trial for treason. The original castle was a square building with six towers and a keep, a design that was gradually becoming inadequate for keeping a determined enemy at bay. Fort Risban, on the other hand, was built by Edward III in the 1340s to protect the sea route into Calais and proved its worth over and over again, right up until the Second World War when it was used as an air-raid shelter. Its remains are to be found in Avenue Raymond Poincaré at the entrance to the port of Calais. Originally known as the 'Lancaster Tower', it had two low towers, specifically designed for the use of artillery. Sluice gates had also been built to control the waters of the Hames, and could be opened to flood the land around the city, deterring attacks from the landward side. Although the lighthouse, nowadays an important landmark, dates only from the nineteenth century, visitors energetic enough to climb to the top will have an excellent panoramic view of the city which may assist in understanding how it was defended in the past.

As they entered the city, Henry must have been happy to see his old friend the Earl of Warwick, who had arranged a suitable reception from the clergy and townspeople, and no doubt one of his first calls was to give thanks at the church of Notre-Dame de Calais, a well-fortified building, where he may have seen some of the colourful wall paintings that were rediscovered in the nineteenth century, having been whitewashed over when the French regained possession of the city. They included several conventional religious images, as well as more secular ones. Around each painting were the words 'Le Jour Viendra' ('The day will come'), repeated many times, apparently the motto of a Thomas Wodehouse who is presumed to have been laid to rest in the church. Major damage was done to Notre-Dame by allied bombing in 1944, and it took around forty years to complete the restoration to the point where there was something for visitors to see, but the work continues into the twenty-first century.

Despite the celebrations for Henry's victorious arrival, Calais in November 1415 was under some pressure. While the nobles stayed in the castle area, the troops had to find makeshift accommodation while awaiting ships to take them back to England. Before two years were up, some of them would find themselves back in the city, preparing for another bloody campaign. (In fact, it would take England that long to finish paying them off for their service at Agincourt.) For the time being, they were more than content to return home for some respite. Henry had them quickly shipped off, but himself remained in Calais for around a fortnight for reasons that are unclear. No doubt, as well as continuing negotiations with the French, he wanted to allow time for his people at home to prepare a suitably elaborate welcome; the anticipation of seeing him return, preceded by the news of his victory, would stir them into a show of patriotism.

*****

When Henry arrived back in England, some time between 15 and 20 November, he was greeted as a national hero. His people had been receiving bad news from the front for some weeks, so the report of the victory at Agincourt had come as a pleasant surprise. The national response might be compared to what English people of today feel on the rare occasions when their cricket team enjoys an unexpected win over Australia. Before he even arrived, the king's brother John, Duke of Bedford, had summoned Parliament to vote more money to the war effort, and Archbishop Chichele had held a convocation of churchmen at St Paul's to raise even more.

After a rough crossing from Calais to Dover, the victorious king was greeted at Barham Down by representatives of the Cinque Ports. They came in such large numbers that the captive Charles d'Orleans, riding alongside him as a trophy, is alleged to have mistaken them for another army and thought that Henry was going straight back to conquer the rest of France. The royal party spent two days at St Augustine's Abbey in Canterbury, the ancient city that had become a centre of English Christianity, the more so since the shrine of Thomas Becket had been installed in the cathedral in the early thirteenth century. Henry made a thank-offering there, and no doubt also visited his father's tomb. The inventory of the gold recovered from the tomb when it was dismantled in 1538 reveals that these included a likeness of Henry, apparently given at some stage in thanks for his recovery from his wound at Shrewsbury.

On arrival at Eltham Palace, still a royal residence, Henry was able to rest only briefly before joining in the celebrations his subjects had prepared for him. At Blackheath, then not part of London, the citizens of the metropolis went out to meet their king, all wearing red. At London Bridge the people had erected a giant figure (complete with an equally hideous wife), which Lydgate described as '...full grim of sight/ To teach the Frenchmen courtesy'.

The tower at Cornhill was covered in red cloth, which sported the arms of St George, St Edward and St Edmund. Men dressed as Biblical characters released a flock of small birds, some of which alighted on the king, a fact not lost on those in search of good omens. At Cheapside, the city's principal commercial district, he was met with a model castle and bridge, and entertained by a choir of white-clad virgins, echoing King David's triumphant return to Jerusalem. The difference between King Henry and King David was that Henry was seen to respond in a quiet, restrained manner to the merry-making.

Eighteen bishops are said to have attended the king at the old St Paul's Cathedral, where he dismounted and visited the tomb of the seventh-century St Earconwald, a former Bishop of London and the capital's patron saint; this was a popular pilgrimage destination. Later, at Westminster Abbey, Henry gave thanks for his victory, laying great emphasis on the religious significance of his experiences. On 1 December, an enormous funeral was held for the Duke of York, doubling as a memorial service for all the dead (on both sides) of the Agincourt campaign. Even the Earl of Dorset made it out of Harfleur in order to attend. A year on from the battle, Henry would be attending a private memorial mass, and would command the Bishop of London to have the feasts of Crispian, Crispinian and his old favourite, St John of Beverley, celebrated on 25 October every year throughout the archdiocese of Canterbury – it would become a 'red-letter day' in the calendar of saints.

Henry proceeded to spend Christmas at Lambeth Palace. In the meantime, the people of France had reacted to the result of the battle with horror and sorrow. Services of mourning were held, and most people, rightly, blamed the battle commanders. There were many accusations of cowardice. Nevertheless, the English gains were minimal. The French were as intransigent as ever, and began to thirst for revenge. This served only to make the King of England more determined.

Chapter 7

Second French Campaign – Rouen and Paris

While a peace was being negotiated, the war continued, off and on, in the English Channel. Almost as soon as Henry had left the country, Harfleur was under pressure from the French once again, besieged both from the sea and the land. It was another of the king's younger brothers, John, Duke of Bedford, who came to the rescue. In the meantime, Henry had an important visitor. Sigismund, the recently-elected Holy Roman Emperor, arrived in England early in the summer of 1416, on a diplomatic mission, and stayed for several months. Formerly an ally of the French, Sigismund now saw England as a safer bet. On the same day that Bedford overcame a French blockade at the mouth of the Seine, a new treaty was signed at Canterbury in Kent, cementing an alliance.

Like Henry, Sigismund had no time for heretics, and it was he who had lured the Czech theologian Jan Hus into attending the Council of Constance (in present-day Germany), as a result of which Hus was tried for heresy and burned at the stake. Sigismund's motive for persuading England and France to settle their differences was an ambition to begin effective crusading in the Middle East again. An end to the Great Schism[2] was in sight, and it was the first time a reigning Holy Roman Emperor had made a state visit to England. Sigismund

---

2. The great Western Schism lasted from 1378 to 1417, during which period two rival popes, one in Rome and one in Avignon, contended for supremacy. In November 1417 Martin V would be elected, putting an end to the dispute.

Second French Campaign – Rouen and Paris

was escorted from Calais by a fleet of 300 ships, but his reception at Dover, by Henry's brother Humphrey, Duke of Gloucester, was not what we might expect today. He was met by Humphrey on the beach and was expected to wade, or ride, ashore from his ship, so as to make it clear that his authority as emperor was suspended while he was in the country. Sigismund obligingly announced that he came as the king's friend, not as emperor.

Sigismund arrived at the beginning of May and was not to leave until 24 August, several weeks after the signing of the treaty. At every stage of his journey from Dover to London, he was greeted by notable men as pre-arranged. Just outside London, Henry came to welcome him personally, with all his brothers in tow, and escorted him through an enormous crowd of spectators to Westminster, where he awarded him the Order of the Garter. Sigismund was given accommodation in Westminster Palace, while Henry himself moved out to make room for the emperor's huge entourage. The king would stay at Lambeth Palace for the duration of the visit. Normally the residence of the Archbishop of Canterbury, Lambeth Palace was not the same building we see today; the palace was largely rebuilt under Tudor rule and again after the Restoration in the seventeenth century. Even its oldest surviving section, the so-called 'Lollards' Tower', was built after the death of Henry V. The archbishop, Henry Chichele, was on good terms with the king and is sometimes credited with having encouraged him to launch the Agincourt campaign. He was a diplomat but also a determined anti-heresy campaigner, responsible for the imprisonment and execution of many Lollards.

Not long after Sigismund, another visitor arrived. This one was William, Duke of Bavaria, brother-in-law and ally of John the Fearless, Duke of Burgundy. William was Count of Holland, Hainaut and Zeeland (all in the Low Countries), and his interest in Henry had more to do with mutual military support than religion. Flanders was a traditional ally of England, and William's grandmother, Margaret, had been the sister of Henry's great-grandmother, Queen Philippa.

However, any advantage either the Duke of Bavaria or the English king might have obtained from their alliance was short-lived; William died about a year later from an infected dog-bite, leaving no male heir.

Before the treaty with Sigismund came negotiations with French ambassadors who had followed the emperor across the Channel. William of Bavaria stayed on long enough to lend his support as an intermediary. Henry again gave his terms for relinquishing his claim to the throne of France, and once again they were refused outright by the French representatives, who declined even to accept the English possession of Harfleur. Their rejection of the offer was Sigismund's excuse to turn against them. Following the signing of his treaty with Henry, the emperor set off for France to hold negotiations with John the Fearless.

The recent events at Harfleur revealed that the French had, at last, managed to accumulate a fleet worthy of the name. The Seine estuary was particularly wide, and a blockade had been highly effective. Even as Sigismund was arriving in the country, the French had been carrying out hit-and-run raids on the south coast of England. Henry was forced to assemble a new fleet, which he had originally planned to lead himself, but reluctantly handed it over to Bedford because of his own state commitments. The fleet assembled at Southampton and Winchelsea, with Lord Hungerford as second-in-command. In a battle that lasted many hours and resulted in heavy casualties, the English were victorious. The news reached Henry at Hythe in Kent, on his way to meet Sigismund at Canterbury, where a celebratory service was held.

Sigismund left from Dover on 25 August; Adam of Usk tells us that he took with him a message, praising the English for their devotion to God and calling them 'blessed'. On 4 September, Henry crossed again to Calais. The purpose of his visit was to join Sigismund in negotiating with the Duke of Burgundy, and the emperor greeted him warmly on the shore. Henry was accompanied by a large entourage, most of whom the castle did not have the space to accommodate. One of his followers, the elderly Lord Morley, only recently appointed Admiral of the King's Ships during the sea engagement at Harfleur, had been with Henry during the Agincourt campaign and was still suffering the after-effects of fever and dysentery. Less than a fortnight after arriving, Morley died and was given a splendid funeral mass at the Church of Notre Dame, in the presence of both Henry and Sigismund, before his body was returned to England for burial.

In October, the negotiations with the Duke of Burgundy finally took place, and lasted a week, but John the Fearless turned out to have his own agenda. Henry V was unusual in often carrying out his own diplomatic missions, and had actually written out some of the negotiating points with his own hand. Perhaps he was suspicious of the duke, even though his father's former ally had obliged him by staying away from Agincourt. John, equally suspicious, had insisted that a suitable hostage be delivered before the negotiations, in order to ensure his personal safety; once again, the job went to Humphrey, Duke of Gloucester. Although the two rulers seem to have come to some kind of understanding, no formal agreement appears to have been signed. John was still hedging his bets. It was left to Sigismund to see Henry off on his journey home.

On his return to England, Henry held another parliament in November, at which the plans for a second invasion of France were approved. Parliament agreed to support his 'unbreakable resolve to go overseas… to subdue the stubborn and more than adamantine obduracy of the French…'. This was just the boost he needed. Meanwhile, there were other matters to attend to at home. Gilbert Talbot, Lord Strange, the elder brother of Henry's friend John Talbot, had been put in charge of the Welsh borders in order to clean up any stray rebels after a pardon had been offered and ignored to the fugitive Owain Glyndŵr. Owain may well have died by this time, but at least one of his sons remained at large. The Scots had also not forgotten past conflicts, and Henry dangled the prospect of an imminent release before the captive King James. All of these actions may be seen as clearing the decks in readiness for Henry's biggest, longest and most successful French campaign.

*****

By the spring of 1417 Henry, who had never stopped building up his military resources, was ready to launch another invasion of France. His good luck continued for a little while: Louis, the Dauphin, had died before the end of 1415, passing his claim to a younger brother, John; the latter was just as sickly as his three elder brothers had been and died in April 1417, further increasing the chances of Henry succeeding to the French throne. By then, the English king was already amassing another fleet and army in readiness for his second incursion into France. The French opposition, gathering in the English Channel, was now reinforced by a fleet of Genoese ships. This time, the man dispatched to sweep them from the sea was the king's first cousin, John Holland, Earl of Huntingdon (recently restored to his father's title after a blip in the family's fortunes during the reign of Henry IV). Once again the English sailors and their allies prevailed. The enemy commander, the 'Bastard of Bourbon' (actually Alexander, an illegitimate son of the Duke of Bourbon), was captured, along with several Genoese ships.

Anticipating further trouble at sea, Henry authorised the building of more warships, notably the enormous *Grace Dieu*, which archaeologists suggest was 'built in a hurry'. Although launched in 1418, it was never used in anger, and was sold off after the king's death. Later, laid up in the River Hamble near Southampton, it was damaged by fire, and the wreck remains in situ, now under the protection of English Heritage. Whether by coincidence or design, the wreck of another of Henry's ships lies nearby: the *Holy Ghost* had actually been captured from the Castilian allies of the French, then renamed and reused as part of the Agincourt fleet.

Now, with the French fleet neutralised, it was time to take advantage of the enemy's continued internal troubles. The preparations were thorough, and the English set sail from Portsmouth on 30 July with an estimated 40,000 men, including soldiers, archers, artillery, and support staff like masons and miners who were essential to the success of any such campaign. To avoid the errors he had made during the early part of the Agincourt campaign, Henry planned to employ the kind of tactics that had succeeded in Wales, the taking of key strongholds en route to his final goal.

This time Henry's forces landed on the beaches near Touques, where a siege of the town's castle began immediately and lasted until 9 August, when he wrote to the people of London with a progress report. The castle, located in the present-day village of Bonneville-sur-Touques, was supposedly the location for William the Conqueror's fateful meeting with Harold Godwinson in 1064, and is still known by locals as the 'Château de Guillaume-le-Conquérant'. What remains of it has been partly converted into a rather grand private house. Henry was the last of several kings of England to have made themselves at home there. The nearby castle of Auvillars was given up, without much resistance, by its lord, Richard de Tournebu. Henry passed it on to his childhood friend Thomas Montagu, Earl of Salisbury, who had negotiated the surrender. That castle is no longer standing.

Henry's brother Thomas, after recovering from a bout of dysentery, proved a vital lieutenant, first taking Lisieux without a fight and then occupying parts of the great city of Caen. Since Henry's accession, the brothers had gradually been reconciled, and by working together at Harfleur, they had re-established a close bond. The taking of Caen was critical to the success of this invasion and would lead to the capitulation of other important towns in Normandy. Its fortifications were impressive, and its twin abbeys had strong defences. Once in English hands, these would prove a stepping-stone to the capture of the citadel itself.

Caen today is popular with British tourists because of the major role it has played in the history of the UK, from the time of the Norman invasion of England right up to the Second World War. The city owed its existence to William the Conqueror, who had founded the abbey of Saint-Étienne (the 'Abbaye aux Hommes') while his wife, Matilda, founded the Abbey of Saint-Trinité (the 'Abbaye aux Dames') a short distance away. William and Matilda were buried at their respective foundations. Caen remained in Anglo-Norman hands until 1204, when it was taken back by the French king, who reinforced the already massive fortifications. King Edward III of England, Henry of Monmouth's great-grandfather, had re-taken it in 1346, looting the city and killing many of its citizens, but had given up on the idea of storming the castle. Henry realised that he could not afford to leave this potential enemy stronghold uncaptured.

It was at the abbey of Saint-Étienne that Henry took up residence while directing the siege. Still one of Normandy's most important buildings, with both Romanesque and Gothic architectural features, it towers over the city. Its ribbed vaulting is the earliest to be found in France, and the extra steeples added in the thirteenth century contribute considerably to the magnificent exterior appearance. Medieval illustrations reveal that there was ample lodging space for the king, and the presence of his most illustrious ancestor's tomb must have been an inspiration to him. Visitors to the church today should be aware that most of the Conqueror's bones went missing in the sixteenth century, although his tomb is still marked.

Caen was partly an island in the River Orne, one branch of which has now been diverted underground. The Isle de St Jean, despite its ancient church of the same name, which still stands, was the 'New Town', created by the building of a canal by William the Conqueror's son Robert. It was connected by a single bridge to the old district where the castle was located. Henry brought with him the materials required to create an additional temporary bridge. Despite his reluctance to damage the older churches with cannon-fire, he had no hesitation in using the towers of the twin abbeys as gun platforms.

Caen fell to Henry's forces after a siege and bombardment lasting over a month. A potential support route from Honfleur, another small port on the Seine estuary, was cut off without the need to launch a siege there. Thomas of Lancaster, the king's brother, now stood in the way of any assistance that might come from the direction of Rouen. The final attack on Caen, on the morning of 4 September, was an all-out assault from two sides of the town walls, one led by the king himself and the other by Thomas. The town was soon in English hands, and the castle garrison lasted out only a few more days before surrendering. The Earl of Ormonde, an ardent supporter, reported to Henry's later biographers that the king had put the city's valuables into storage and entrusted the care of them to his brother Thomas. Notwithstanding this testimony, it is known that there was considerable looting and unnecessary slaughter when Caen was taken.

The outcome of the 1417 siege was only marginally less damaging than that of 1346, entailing an estimated 2,000 civilian deaths. Henry justified the deaths of so many citizens by means of passages from the Old Testament Book of Deuteronomy: if the people of a town fail to surrender to the army of God's chosen people when they have the chance, and a siege ensues, it is acceptable – indeed mandatory – for the conqueror to put the male population to the sword and take everything else as booty. The lives of women, children and priests were normally spared, and Henry's preferred resolution was always simply to evict French natives from the city and replace them with English volunteer settlers. In this case, it may have been his intention to frighten other towns into surrendering without a fight. With Caen in his hands, Henry had a suitable base to fall back on during the winter if necessary.

Over the next three years, Henry's armies did considerable damage to France's defences. As he had hoped, the fall of Caen encouraged other towns in Normandy to give way gracefully. When the ever-useful Duke of Gloucester approached Bayeux, the town offered no resistance, and Argentan was next to go, on 8 October. It was at Argentan that Henry set up a temporary headquarters. He had no desire to continue to demolish fortifications for the sake of it; on the contrary, he wanted every French town populated by loyal citizens to bolster his rule throughout the land when, as he anticipated, his claim to the throne was accepted. Those modern critics who have dubbed Henry a warmonger have often been the same ones who complain that his efforts were in vain because he failed to subdue the whole of France. Yet it is difficult to see how he could have done otherwise than conquer such a large country piecemeal, just as the Normans had done with England and Wales in the 200 years after the Battle of Hastings.

Bayeux remains popular with British tourists because of the presence of the Bayeux 'tapestry', a 230-foot long embroidery depicting the Norman conquest of England, which has its own museum. Traditionally supposed to have been made by attendants of William the Conqueror's queen, Matilda, the embroidery may have been made in England but seems to have been specifically designed to fit the cathedral at Bayeux, where it was regularly exhibited over the centuries. It is no longer held there, but is displayed under protected conditions at the Musée de la Tapisserie.

The city, originally a Roman settlement on the River Aure, had been fought over almost incessantly between the death of Richard the Lionheart and the arrival of Henry V. Other than the Norman cathedral, rebuilt over the centuries so that the exterior looks very different, relatively few medieval buildings survive. There is, however, a nineteenth-century statue of one of the town's most notable sons, Alain Chartier, a poet and political analyst of around Henry's own age, whose service as secretary to the new Dauphin, Charles, became invaluable. Chartier was the author of the *Livre des quatre dames* (1416), a poem of courtly love that references the events of the Battle of Agincourt.

Argentan, a city of a similar size to Bayeux, is less familiar to overseas visitors. In the course of the air raids around 'D-Day' in

1944, the town was almost completely destroyed, and there is little surviving of the medieval settlement that Henry knew. The massive 'donjon', or castle keep, is reputed to have been built by King Henry II of England, a distant ancestor of Henry of Monmouth, and remains impressive. By the time Henry saw it, subsequent owners had added the 'Grand Logis', turning it into a comfortable residence fit for a king. Though much altered, the building can still be seen, and now houses the law courts.

Anyone visiting Argentan needs to be aware of the extent of the damage done to it during the Second World War. The 'Tour Marguerite', a stout defensive structure, although named after a seventeenth-century princess, is the only remaining part of Argentan's medieval city walls; it has been subject to prettification. Both the tower and the castle are open to the public, and offer the visitor spectacular views over the town. Henry spent over a week in residence at the 'Château des Ducs' in October 1417, looking out from a similar viewpoint, gathering intelligence, and taking time to decide what his next move should be.

Henry moved on quickly to take personal charge of the siege of Alençon. The nominal Duke of Alençon, whose father had died at Agincourt, was eight years old and not in a position to offer any resistance or assist the citizens; the town was in English hands by 22 October. Here it was that the king received a visit from his stepbrother, John, Duke of Brittany. Becoming anxious about the English army's increasing proximity to his own territory, John was eager to offer himself as a potential ally. The two leaders signed an extended truce, but Henry would have been mindful that John was married to one of the Dauphin's sisters and his loyalty was always suspect.

John's younger brother, Arthur, who would succeed him as Duke of Brittany, was moreover still a prisoner in England, albeit in comfortable conditions, and Arthur had been a bosom friend of the late Dauphin Louis (whose widow he would marry after his eventual release). Perhaps it was because of this that Henry was beginning to doubt the wisdom of allowing freedom of movement to John's mother, Joanna, the widow of Henry IV, who was confined to Pevensey Castle on trumped-up charges not long afterwards.

Falaise, the birthplace of William the Conqueror, with the next strongest defences in the region after those of Caen, was Henry's next target, but he does not seem to have been in any great hurry, probably because he was watching and waiting for news of the latest developments within the French kingdom, as well as taking stock of worrying news from home; the Scots had again infiltrated England's northern borders. Midway through November, the news came that the French court had relocated to Troyes.

Falaise was well-defended, its castle even more so. Visitors today still have a steep climb to arrive at the castle gate and view the daunting spectacle of this immense fortress from close quarters. The River Ante below was a second line of defence, but on the other side of the ravine were even taller cliffs, and it was here, on Mont Myrrha (perhaps 'mons mirabilis'), that Henry positioned his artillery. This area can be explored on foot, and in places climbed (but only by the suitably experienced).

Within the walls of the castle, restored in the late twentieth century and reopened to visitors in 1997, are audio-visual displays that concentrate mainly on the period of the Dukes of Normandy and early Norman kings. Like the castle at Bonneville-sur-Touques, it is popularly known as 'Château de Guillaume-le-Conquérant'. The castle was a bone of contention throughout the Hundred Years' War, but fell out of use in the seventeenth century and was practically a ruin by the mid-nineteenth century when the French government began to conserve its historic monuments. In its restored state, it gives an excellent idea of what Henry V was up against. Accordingly, he did not bother to try to storm the town, which was taken in December 1417 after a short siege.

The French had already sent peace negotiators to invite the English king to a conference at Barneville, near Honfleur, but discussions ended quickly when Henry made it clear he would drop none of his demands. If the French approach was intended as a distraction, it failed, and Henry quickly returned to business. With great practicality, he had protected his besieging force from the elements by housing the men in temporary huts at Falaise, and, with characteristic foresight, he ensured that the town could be held by his garrison for as long as required, by forcing the occupants to rebuild the walls at their own expense. Once again, the decisive move was a three-pronged attack by Henry's brothers, Thomas and Humphrey, and his friend the Earl of Salisbury. The castle held out for an additional month, but capitulated after mining and artillery had done sufficient damage. Henry himself remained in Falaise until Easter 1418, moving on to Bayeux to celebrate the holy days.

By April 1418, Henry's reconquest of Normandy was more or less complete, with so many towns and cities already in his hands and reinforcements arriving from home. Thomas and Humphrey had proved effective deputies, as had his friends the earls of Salisbury, Warwick and Huntingdon, mopping up the remaining opposition. Huntingdon had taken Coustances and Avranches, while Thomas took Courtonne, Riviere-Thibouville and Chambrais. Humphrey had been involved in the capture of Carentan and St-Sauveur. Henry's uncle, the Earl of Dorset, had been created Duke of Exeter in recognition of his faithful service, and now repaid his nephew by taking the cathedral city of Évreux. For the time being, there was little left for the king to do except perfect his strategy for expansion.

After Easter, Henry returned to Caen where he celebrated St George's Day ostentatiously, doling out knighthoods in the citadel. Meanwhile, Humphrey set off to lay siege to the port of Cherbourg, at the head of the Cotentin peninsula; most of the peninsula was already in English hands. Cherbourg held out for five months, but was worth the trouble because it was well-supplied with the stores the English forces could use.

Thomas's energies were occupied in helping his brother prepare for the assault on Rouen, France's second city and the capital of the duchy of Normandy. There was one problem – John the Fearless, Duke of Burgundy, having overcome the Armagnac opposition, was now offering assistance to the besieged city, despite his informal agreement with Henry. Legates from the new pope had approached both sides of the Armagnac/Burgundy dispute in an attempt to make peace between the rival French factions. Fortunately for Henry, Bernard VII of Armagnac, Burgundy's sworn enemy, turned down these overtures, and by the end of May, the Burgundians had taken Paris. This left Henry free to meet up with his brother Thomas at Bernay, a small town in the Charentonne valley.

Bernay, though relatively unimportant in the grand scheme of things, has been designated one of France's Villes et Pays d'Art et d'Histoire (Towns and Lands of Art and History), on account of its eleventh-century Benedictine abbey and the many half-timbered houses that survive, surrounding the town's market square. A centre of cloth-making in the Middle Ages, it now possesses a highly-rated museum, located in what was once the abbot's residence and containing artefacts from all periods of the town's history.

In June 1418, the immediate target of the English was Louviers, a well-defended town about twenty miles from Rouen. Louviers had been sacked twice by King Edward III and the Black Prince, but the townspeople had since rebuilt their walls as well as constructing a new church; they were still working on Notre-Dame de Louviers when the English arrived, but it was a much simpler building than the one a present-day visitor will see, since many changes to the original design were made later in the fifteenth century, resulting in an outstanding example of the 'Flamboyant Gothic' architectural style. The Challenge Tower, which had been begun in 1414, was a deliberately robust fortified structure, intended as a bell-tower but also as a potential refuge in times of conflict. It was restored during the 2010s and is still prominent at the western end of the church.

The siege of Louviers lasted only a week, by the end of which the English had breached the walls with the assistance of a new siege engine reputedly designed by the king himself. Henry supervised the siege personally, and it was here, according to John Strecche, a priest from Kenilworth who recorded the event, that he had a close encounter with death, when a gun-stone hit the exact spot where he had been standing a second earlier. The king 'gratefully gave thanks to God who had saved him', no doubt taking this as additional evidence of the rightness of his cause. Nor would his death have meant the end of English aggression, with Thomas, the heir presumptive to the English throne, on the spot.

After a short battle, the authorities gave in gracefully, but the captain of the guard did not escape with his life. He had been involved in previous resistance and had gone back on a promise not to fight against Henry again, so he was put to death along with the team of gunners who had almost knocked the king's head off. Louviers gave Henry easier access to the crossing of the Seine at Pont de l'Arche, where a Burgundian force was spotted on the opposite bank, ready to prevent the English from crossing by the bridge which controlled the river traffic. Henry's practical nature and foresight were once again in evidence: his troops used small boats and pontoon bridges to cross at night, with some small islands in the river as stepping-stones, and managed to take the opposition by surprise. Nevertheless, it took until 20 July to capture the 'stately' castle.

Once Warwick and Salisbury had returned from their travels, they set off with Henry, taking less than a day to reach Rouen. On arrival there, the king once again moved into monastic lodgings nearby while supervising the siege. The Charterhouse or Carthusian monastery of Notre Dame de la Rose, founded in 1346, was a relatively new building, and its position made it highly suitable as a place from which to view the action and supply the besiegers. No trace of it remains, but it is believed to have stood in the vicinity of the road known as Rue de la Petite Chartreuse, which is now in a mostly commercial/industrial area of the city.

Just as at Harfleur, Henry set up palisades to protect his artillery, as is demonstrated in a fifteenth-century illustration from a manuscript that seems to have originated from the family of his great friend the Earl of Warwick, who is depicted supervising the siege along with the king. They constructed siege towers and a ditch around the town, containing various hazards. Nevertheless, the people of Rouen withstood a siege of six months before they gave way. The city was exceptionally well-defended and well-supplied, and initially expected assistance from the Duke of Burgundy. The English, with assistance from their Portuguese allies, managed to cut off access from the river Seine, and no further help arrived from the Burgundians. Meanwhile, Henry ordered provisions from London, 'especially drink'.

Many of Henry's lieutenants during this siege were veterans of the Agincourt campaign: in addition to Warwick and Salisbury, he could count on support from his uncle Exeter, his cousin Huntingdon, the Duke of Norfolk (who had been sent home with dysentery from Harfleur, but was now fighting fit) and Sir Thomas Erpingham. The contributions of Sir Robert Babthorpe, known as the 'King's Controller', would prove vital to the success of the siege. Babthorpe, a Yorkshire knight who had been a member of the royal household since 1406, seems to have been an accomplished engineer. He would be an executor of Henry V's will and would go on to serve the next king.

While the siege continued, Henry's brother Humphrey finally succeeded in taking Cherbourg, and Salisbury moved a few miles upriver to take possession of the Benedictine abbey of Sainte-Catherine du Mont, a fortified monastery that was occupied by the French. They surrendered on 1 September, but the danger of an enemy force arriving to relieve Rouen had not been removed. John the Fearless was still attempting to negotiate with the Dauphin Charles (who incidentally was still only fifteen years old). Charles had fled Paris, but while he prevaricated, no action was taken. By October, officials from Rouen had gone to the capital to make a direct appeal to the government, and were promised relief. On their return, they relayed the good news to the citizens, and all the church bells

Second French Campaign – Rouen and Paris

in the city were rung. Unknown to them, both the Duke of Burgundy and the Dauphin had been holding on-and-off negotiations with the English behind the scenes, and no relief force ever turned up.

John the Fearless had in fact raised an army, which was encamped at Pontoise, on the outskirts of Paris, for several weeks in November. Embarrassed by the failure of the French government to negotiate effectively, John eventually let his troops go and withdrew to the borders of his own duchy, while the Dauphin sent ambassadors to Henry, cap-in-hand, seeking a summit meeting between the two rival claimants to the French throne. They arrived just in time to watch Rouen surrender on 19 January.

When all the animals inside the walls had been killed and eaten, the men of Rouen had sent thousands of their women, children and other non-combatants outside the gates, believing that Henry would be chivalrous enough to let them go. Unexpectedly, perhaps provoked by the actions of the officials in Rouen, who had been hanging English prisoners from the ramparts, Henry instructed his army not to let them pass, and most died of starvation in a defensive ditch outside the castle walls. Heavy rain lasting several weeks exacerbated their plight. The action won the king no friends amongst the opposition, and left a stain on his reputation. However, it was only after he took Rouen and started threatening Paris that the French government finally capitulated.

At Christmas, there was a brief truce, during which Henry, according to some accounts, distributed food to the few surviving people in the ditches outside the walls. Then he returned to his own quarters to dine on roast porpoise and other delicacies. Perhaps the sight of even a small amount of food was a factor in the eventual decision of the people of Rouen to give up their struggle. As usual, Henry received the surrender from a point deliberately selected to emphasise his advantage. Guy de Bouteiller, the French garrison commander who had led the resistance, was obliged to bring the keys of the city to the king at the Chartreuse where he was lodging, along with a negotiated payment of £50,000. Within the city walls, the English standard was displayed on every available surface, and the following day the remaining men of the garrison were allowed to march out unharmed, but forfeited all their possessions, including any spare clothing. Meanwhile, having ridden out from the Chartreuse, the king himself entered through a different gate, to the sound of church bells and celebratory cannon.

On this occasion, looting and bloodshed were kept to a minimum, and Henry had already had food brought into the city by Candlemas, which he celebrated there, foiling an assassination attempt timed for what was then an important religious festival marking the end of the Christmas season. Robert de Linet, the 'vicar-general' of Rouen, who had made a grand performance of excommunicating Henry from the city walls, was now a prisoner, kept under harsher conditions than the devout king would normally have imposed on a priest.

It was the continued hostility between the Armagnacs and Burgundians that had enabled Henry to make so much headway. Charles VI's queen consort, Isabeau of Bavaria, who had begun by siding with Burgundy but had diplomatically (she thought) gone over to the Armagnacs, was a prime mover in the conflict. Isabeau, a foreign-born consort with an incapable husband, was vulnerable; she was said to be the lover of John the Fearless, and was even prepared to allow the Dauphin Charles to be declared illegitimate in order to consolidate her position. While Henry had been marching on Rouen, the Burgundians had stormed Paris and taken control, and the future of the kingdom of France remained in the balance. Many of the inhabitants of Rouen, angry with the way their own leaders had let them down, were only too ready to swear an oath of allegiance to Henry in order to be allowed to remain.

*****

Rouen, the capital of Normandy, is a city familiar to many British travellers. Its centre retains many medieval buildings, notably the great cathedral, already established by the seventh century. Many additions and alterations have been made over the centuries - the depredations of the revolutionary years, lightning strikes and hurricanes have all played their part, and the building we see now is not as Henry would have seen it. It would nevertheless have been impressive, containing the tombs of his ancestors, the Empress Matilda (mother of King Henry II) and William Longsword, one of the first rulers of an independent Normandy, not to mention the heart of another English warrior king, Richard the Lionheart.

The abbey church of St Ouen, begun in 1318, was far from complete when Henry V passed through Rouen. Its construction had been repeatedly interrupted by the wars between France and England. The later additions to St Ouen clearly show the influence of English architecture, specialist craftspeople having been recruited from Paris to work on it. Meanwhile, the church of St Maclou that then stood was a relatively small Norman church, not the Gothic edifice that now stands on the site.

The Gros Horloge, an astronomical clock, is one of the most popular attractions in Rouen, and was in the process of construction in Henry's day, with the intention of replacing a belfry that had been destroyed by the French king in 1382 as punishment for the 'Harelle', a revolt against high taxes that was almost contemporary with the Peasants' Revolt in England. The clock would originally have had no dial, and was located in a different spot, in the belfry next to the Renaissance arch where it now has pride of place over one of Rouen's busiest thoroughfares.

On arrival in Rouen, Henry announced his intention to build himself a new palace there, emphasising his status as Duke of Normandy, although technically the treaty he had signed did not give him that status. He even wore an outfit decorated with the arms of the duchy, but he must have been aware that many of the citizens who had been there during the previous summer's siege would not yet have forgiven him for their ordeal. Henry began work on his palace in 1419 and it was continued by his younger brother Bedford in the years after the king's death. In 1429, after Bedford became regent, he made Rouen his base, but the new palace was not finished until 1449, when the French were very much back in control of their capital city. The palace stood in the Rue de Vieux Palais and the Place Henri IV, an area that was completely redeveloped in the 16th century but suffered further damage during the revolutionary period. The palace itself was demolished in 1792, although some medieval remains can still be seen.

The Rue du Vieux Palais passes close to the magnificent modern church of Sainte-Jeanne-d'Arc. It is perhaps fitting that Joan of Arc, who would lead future campaigns against the English, should be commemorated so close to the transient seat of Henry's power. The bishop's palace that stood near the cathedral in 1418 was demolished a few decades later by a new archbishop, and rebuilt. Part of it has found a new use and is open to the public. Joan of Arc was still a small child when Henry began the task of conquering France, and her name was then unknown. As befits her current status, she became the subject of a large modern museum in 2015, replacing the tiny old-fashioned waxwork museum that closed in 2012. Although the Historial Jeanne d'Arc, located at the site of her trial in the former archdiocesan buildings, deals mostly with the period after Henry's death, its interactive displays help the visitor imbibe the atmosphere of the fifteenth century and the Hundred Years' War.

All that remains of Rouen's Norman castle is the keep, often called 'Joan of Arc's Tower' – more to attract tourists than because of any close association with the saint herself. Joan was certainly imprisoned in the castle prior to her execution in 1431, but not in this tower. Although the tower was remodelled in the nineteenth century, by which time the rest of the castle had been demolished, its size and shape give some idea of how strong the fortifications were. The royal apartments in Rouen Castle included a chapel and several private chambers, with a main staircase leading to the chapel, used

Second French Campaign – Rouen and Paris

intensively by Henry. He also converted the 'great chamber' into a kind of kitchen/diner, himself sleeping in a neighbouring chamber with en suite facilities.

Henry immediately began finalising the details of his rule over Normandy by confirming the charters of all its major towns, including Caen, Harfleur and Rouen itself, as they already stood, thus highlighting the extent of his territory and demonstrating that he was legally replacing the French king as ruler rather than taking the lands by force. As those antipathetic to Anglo-Norman rule began to emigrate from the duchy, others who were more sympathetic would begin to return from exile.

*****

With Rouen in Henry's possession, other Norman towns began to fall like skittles, with little military force required. By the middle of February 1419, even places Henry had previously avoided attacking, like Montivilliers, Dieppe and Eu, had given way. The port of Honfleur had been brought into submission by a blockade. A few fortresses remained out of his grasp: Mont-Saint-Michel, uniquely placed on its tidal island, would never surrender. However, the four remaining strongholds – Château Gaillard (famously built by King Richard I of England, 'the Lionheart'), La Roche-Guyon, Gisors and Ivry – were all successfully besieged in the coming months.

The siege of Château Gaillard was particularly time-consuming. Richard had built it to last; after his death, it had held out for six months against Philip II of France, and it had later been used as a secure prison for two adulterous French queens. On this occasion, the siege lasted even longer, and apparently came to an end for the prosaic reason that there were no ropes left to draw water from the well. It was many months before it fell into the hands of the Duke of Exeter, who was supervising operations. Even today, in its ruinous state, it is apparent from a visit to Château Gaillard that the 'saucy castle' presented a significant obstacle to the would-be attacker, and in the end it was a sixteenth-century French king who would order it to be dismantled because of its potential to be used against him (just as Richard had intended). The outer bailey can be visited all year round.

Henry had already begun consolidating his rule of Normandy, reorganising the administration of the duchy and issuing his own coinage. He had made himself familiar with the way it had traditionally been governed under his ancestors, and had trusted Englishmen ready to take over key roles such as Chancellor and Treasurer. There was also a Welshman, the redoubtable Philip Morgan, who had served as Henry's chaplain and had skills in canon law and diplomacy. Henry appointed him Chancellor in April 1418; by the end of 1419, he had been consecrated Bishop of Worcester, at a ceremony in Rouen Cathedral. The duchy promised to provide chosen followers like these with a tidy income and take some of the tax burden off the people of England. In September of that year, the king issued an order preventing English merchants and soldiers from buying large quantities of wine in Normandy. It is interesting to speculate that private individuals were already taking advantage of the opportunities for duty-free trading.

It had come to the point where the king had too many activities on his plate to be able to supervise all the sieges himself, and he entrusted the earls of Salisbury and Huntingdon with consolidating some of his earlier gains. At Fresnay-sur-Sarthe in March, Salisbury's siege was challenged by a French army from Le Mans, reinforced by Scottish troops, and it was Huntingdon who fought them off, though outnumbered. The French were as over-confident as they had been at Agincourt, and their losses were heavy. The exact site of this encounter is as yet unknown, but Fresnay was another of those strategically-important strongholds that changed hands frequently in the course of the Anglo-French wars.

The French were now ready to come to terms. In March, Henry had been invited to meet the Dauphin Charles at Évreux, but Charles had failed to turn up, effectively putting himself out of the picture as far as a peaceful settlement went. Henry spent a few days at Évreux before moving on. The Tour de l'Horloge in the city centre was a new building, constructed less than ten years earlier, and its bell had been named after the Dauphin Louis. Nevertheless, it was almost completely rebuilt towards the end of the century. The cathedral of Notre-Dame d'Évreux was also in the process of reconstruction in the Gothic style, the previous building having been burned down, and work continued despite the English occupation. A new bell-tower had only just been completed, but a couple of centuries later a second tower was added to the west front, whilst the first was unsympathetically crowned with a dome that is quite out of keeping with the rest of the building, so that today's cathedral is not as attractive to the visitor as it might have looked to Henry V.

The abbey of St Taurin, dedicated to Saint Taurinus (reputedly the first bishop of Évreux), retains its medieval features, including a magnificent thirteenth-century reliquary built to contain the saint's remains. The latter was for many years housed in the cathedral, where Henry would no doubt have seen it. The bishop's palace that adjoins the cathedral, now the city museum, was not built for another eighty years or so. It contains an assortment of historical artefacts from all periods of Évreux's history.

Yet again, Henry spent the 2019 Easter holiday in Normandy, this time at Vernon-sur-Seine, about halfway between Rouen and Paris. Today Vernon is about half the size of Évreux, and retains the keep of its castle, now known as the 'Tour des Archives'. This was built by King Henry I of England and is unusual in being a round tower, not dissimilar to 'Joan of Arc's tower' at Rouen. The historic town centre retains many half-timbered buildings, the oldest of which, the 'Maison du Temps Jadis' ('House of Olden Times'), was built in about 1450 and therefore outwardly resembles many of the residential buildings that would have been present when Henry V arrived in town. It survived the Second World War unscathed, and now contains the local tourist information office. On the opposite bank of the Seine, the Château des Tourelles, built by King Philip II of France in the twelfth century, is virtually unchanged in its external appearance, but the interior is not open to the public.

Throughout this period, Henry was busying himself with administrative tasks, such as appointing Warwick his chief ambassador to the French king and Salisbury his 'lieutenant in Normandy'. The negotiations for his marriage to Princess Catherine continued throughout May. Between May and August, Henry based himself at Mantes, near Meulan-en-Yvelines. The senior members of the French royal family were resident at Pontoise, about fifteen miles away from Meulan, which was the neutral territory where vital negotiations would take place. Château Gaillard remained under siege while the negotiations took place, and would not surrender until December 1419.

Mantes, which stands on the Seine about thirty miles west of Paris, was where Philip II had died nearly 200 years earlier, which may have brought to mind the successes of Henry's ancestors but would also have reminded him that Philip eventually got the better of both Richard I and King John. The city had surrendered to the English in February. The remains of the medieval bridge across the Seine have now been incorporated into a new footbridge that runs alongside the newer crossing from Mantes to Limay. The nearby church of Notre-Dame de Mantes, however, continues to dominate the town. Although the north tower was not completed until later in the fifteenth century, the church has broadly the same appearance as it would have when Henry stayed here. The chapel of Navarre had been constructed only about fifty years earlier, and although damaged during the French Revolution, it retains its original appearance. The castle and citadel of Mantes were demolished during the seventeenth century, and any useful building materials were used in the construction of a convent at Limay, of which there is now little trace.

*****

Second French Campaign – Rouen and Paris

It was nearly five years after the victory at Agincourt that King Charles of France finally accepted Henry's demands and made him his heir, at the expense of yet another of his own sons. Queen Isabeau had recently become enthusiastic about the idea of a marriage between her youngest surviving daughter and the King of England, and Henry was finally brought together with his future bride, Catherine of Valois, at Meulan at the end of May 1419, when his rule of Normandy was becoming firmly established. Contemporary accounts suggest that, on meeting Catherine for the first time, Henry was charmed. At any rate, he agreed to dispense with the need for a dowry. We cannot assume that Catherine was equally enthusiastic about her suitor. She was now nineteen years old to Henry's battle-scarred thirty-two. Isabeau shrewdly refused his request for a second meeting; keeping him waiting was bound to increase his impatience to marry, as well as giving the queen time to deal with any doubts her daughter may have expressed.

Almost immediately after the marriage negotiations, John the Fearless, who had been present at Meulan, attempted to make yet another truce with the Dauphin, Charles. Henry had not been fooled by the Duke of Burgundy's promises at Meulan. As soon as Burgundy departed, he headed for Pontoise, a strongly-defended town in a strategic position, sometimes called 'the key to Paris'." It was only a short time since the French royal family had used it as a safe base while negotiations took place at Meulan. The English forces and their Gascon allies attacked under cover of night, and succeeded in scaling the walls and opening the gates, saving considerable time and avoiding bloodshed. Survivors hurried to bring the news to Paris, thus spreading fear throughout the population and assisting Henry's campaign to frighten French towns into submission. The capture of Pontoise also put substantial additional stores at Henry's disposal. It was this event that finally persuaded John the Fearless to try to make peace with the Dauphin in September. His apparent purpose was to exclude Henry from the picture, and it might have been disastrous for the English had not John the Fearless been murdered at the meeting point by a Breton knight, probably with the Dauphin's collusion. This was the end of any hopes of reconciliation between the two French factions.

It was some time during that summer that Henry devised his 'Ordinances of War', a set of rules for the conduct of military campaigns, intended to reinforce discipline and prevent the worst excesses of his soldiers' behaviour. It may seem rather late in the day for him to have been issuing these, bearing in mind all that he had already done, and they were probably a later version of rules he had previously issued during the Agincourt campaign. That he felt moved to reiterate them now suggests a continued concern to ensure that he did not incur any more resentment than necessary among the French people over whom he expected shortly to be ruling.

By the time John the Fearless met his end at Montereau, Henry was residing temporarily at Gisors, around forty miles from Paris, which had just been captured by the English; in the months after John's murder, Henry was everywhere. According to his English biographer, 'almost no day passed but he ...visited some of the towns and strongholds...'. He had taken up residence in the town while the castle at Gisors was still under siege. Largely built by two of the Conqueror's sons, Henry I and William II of England, to defend their territory from the French, the octagonal keep still stands on its motte, making it one of the best-preserved of the many regained by Henry V during his invasion of Normandy. It was protected by a wide moat, but it could not withstand the siege for more than another week, and the garrison capitulated in late September. By the time ambassadors arrived from the French court to continue negotiations, Henry was confident enough to renew his demands, counting on the collapse of Burgundian resistance.

It was in Henry's interests to make peace with the new Duke of Burgundy, twenty-three-year-old Philip 'the Good', and he duly did so. He was in a commanding position, having taken Pontoise in anticipation of neutralising any threat from the Burgundians; he made the city his new base. Now he wanted Paris, and his brother Thomas had already made threatening movements in that direction. News of the capture of Pontoise had caused the French royal family to flee Paris. Philip gave up any designs he may have had on the French crown, and after long and tortuous negotiations, an agreement was reached on 2 December, when Philip recognised Henry as the rightful heir to the French throne. As a sweetener, Henry was offering the marriage of his brother John, Duke of Bedford, to Philip's sister Anne.

A truce with the French was agreed by Christmas 1419, which Henry spent in Rouen while negotiations continued with Philip the Good; on Christmas Day, he sealed that deal. The Dauphin was not out of the picture, though. He had not signed the truce and the English and Burgundians were free to continue to move against him, but at the same time he still had the support of the Scots, as well as of the southern half of France. Nevertheless, the prospects for Henry were much rosier than they had been in the same place at the same time a year earlier.

Henry stayed in Rouen, still occupying himself with administrative matters, until April 1420, when he travelled to Mantes. A few weeks later, he moved on to revisit Pontoise. The city gets its name from the bridge over the River Oise which contributed to the prosperity that Pontoise enjoyed from the twelfth century onwards. The desirability of this location was a double-edged sword for the inhabitants, who barely knew from one day to the next whether they were under French, English or Burgundian rule. Favoured by 'Saint' Louis, the city was dominated by a substantial castle that was one of the linch-pins in Henry's plan to dominate northern France.

Some fragmentary ruins of the castle and town walls remain on the hillside, and can be viewed by visitors; this location should not be confused with the 'Parc du Chateau' in the Rue du Chateau, which relates to a different, later, castle. The cathedral of Saint-Maclou de Pontoise includes architectural elements from various centuries, but is essentially medieval. It had already required a substantial rebuild in the previous century as a result of hurricane damage, and work would continue on and off throughout the fourteenth and fifteenth centuries.

From Troyes to Paris

In May 1420, in accordance with their diplomatic agreement, Henry V left Pontoise and Philip the Good left Paris, both heading for the city of Troyes; they met face to face, for the first time, en route. Like Henry's own court, the French court sometimes moved around the country, but it had been forced to relocate to Troyes when Henry began to threaten Paris, and the royal family no longer had access to the kind of luxuries to which they had been accustomed. They were at a disadvantage when faced with the powerful leaders of England and Burgundy.

Henry avoided the centre of Paris on his way from Pontoise to Troyes, a journey of well over a hundred miles, but did call in to pray at the Abbey of Saint-Denis, the traditional resting-place of the French kings, in what are now the northern suburbs. He travelled via Brie, Charenton, Provins, and Nogent. His progress was impressive, leaving guards behind him at all the bridges on the River Marne, in a show of military strength. He arrived in great state, as did Philip, humbling the French royal family.

One of those now backing Henry was a former enemy of both England and Burgundy, Arthur of Richemont, whose friend the Dauphin Louis was long dead. Following his release from prison in England, he proved valuable during the negotiations, helping to persuade his elder brother, the Duke of Brittany, to sign a peace treaty. As a reward, Arthur would later be given his own dukedom by the English, but after Henry's death the good relations would quickly peter out and he would return to serving the French king.

The Treaty of Troyes, sometimes called the 'New Peace' as distinct from the peace established by King Edward III in 1360, made

Henry regent (this was necessary for the periods when the French king's mental state prevented him from carrying out his normal duties) and acknowledged the children of his marriage to the French princess as the heirs to the French crown. Charles had already been persuaded to disinherit his namesake son, on the dubious grounds of the latter's role in the death of John the Fearless.

When he came into the presence of the queen and the princess (the king being ill and unable to attend), Henry 'bowed very low' to Catherine and 'kissed her with great joy' (according to a French chronicler). An account of their meeting states that he was wearing full armour, with a fox's tail attached to his helmet in place of the usual plume; its significance in the context of this encounter is unclear. The treaty was signed on 21 May 1420, and the couple were betrothed on the same day in Troyes cathedral, where Henry is said to have given his fiancée a ring 'of inestimable value'.[3] The marriage ceremony took place on 2 June, Trinity Sunday, at the Church of St Jean, to which Henry made a generous donation of 200 nobles. The festivities, though no doubt lavish, were short-lived, which could be taken as an omen since their marriage would not be a long one; it would last just long enough for Catherine to give birth to their only child, a son, who would become Henry VI.

During the celebrations, Henry showed his abstemious side by commanding that his men drank only watered-down wine. The army had to be ready to march on 3 June, the day after the wedding. By 5 June, they would be laying siege to the city of Sens. The Archbishop of Sens, Henri de Savoisy, was present at the wedding ceremony and was called upon to bless the marriage bed. Savoisy had been selected by Pope Martin V over a rival claimant in 1418, following the death of his predecessor at the Battle of Agincourt, but had been rejected as a candidate by the city's rulers, and was unable to access his city

---

3. John Speed

because of the Dauphin's presence there. This made a good pretext for leaving Troyes as a matter of urgency. Henry even dispensed with the customary tournament.

The wedding night was spent in the traditional manner. As in England, the couple were seen off to bed by their courtiers, who accompanied them with merry-making. Wine and soup were brought along to fortify them, as was the French royal custom. The ostensible purpose of the public bedding was to verify that the marriage had been consummated and to demonstrate that any children subsequently born to Catherine were legitimate, but the onlookers would normally leave discreetly as soon as the couple got into bed.

Troyes, originally a Roman town, nowadays contains many half-timbered buildings dating from the century after Henry, and it is possible to imagine how the city would have looked in 1420. The medieval cathedral – where the Treaty of Troyes was signed – has only one tower, not because of the considerable damage done to it over the centuries but because the second was never completed. There was, however, a steeple, which was finally destroyed by lightning in 1700. The elaborate west front was not constructed for about another hundred years after the treaty. While visiting the cathedral, Henry would surely have been shown one of its prized possessions, the so-called 'Troyes Casket', a Byzantine royal treasure captured (or, more accurately, stolen) by Crusaders in Constantinople in 1204 and brought to the city by its bishop.

There were two monastic establishments at Troyes. The convent of Notre-Dame-aux-Nonnains, which stood in the Place de la Préfecture, is long since demolished. The only building remaining from the ninth-century Abbey of Saint-Loup (which was destroyed during the French Revolution) is now the home of the city's Musée des Beaux-Arts. At least four of the churches now standing in Troyes were already built in Henry's time. The oldest of these is Ste Madeleine, built in the thirteenth century and later extended from a modest parish church to a more substantial building with a tower. Its chapel dedicated to Saint Louis (King Louis IX of France) is also a later addition.

There can be little doubt that the terms of the Treaty of Troyes were generally unpopular with the French. Some key towns ignored it and refused to acknowledge Henry as their overlord, and he was obliged to continue his war with the Dauphin Charles. He took his new wife with him when he marched west to Sens, which capitulated after a week and a half. Sens, a former capital of the Gauls, was actually a Burgundian town that had fallen into the hands of the Dauphin. As so often happened, the town was quickly taken by the English, but its citadel resisted capture, and Henry, therefore, sent prisoners to plead with the commander for their lives. When they returned without achieving a surrender, perhaps hoping for clemency, they were put to death. Parts of the ramparts that Henry eventually conquered on 11 June can still be seen. In some places, they date from the Merovingian period or even earlier. The medieval layout of the city streets, with the cathedral as their central focus, is very clear from a map or aerial view.

The cathedral of Saint-Étienne de Sens was an important centre of religion, whose archbishop, Henri de Savoisy, had been one of the priests officiating at the king's wedding. It was therefore a point of honour for Henry to restore him to his archdiocese. It is claimed that Henry marked the occasion with the rather glib statement: 'You gave me my wife, and now I give you back yours.' The cathedral is notable for its collection of stained-glass windows, the earliest of which depicts scenes from the life of St Thomas Becket, who had for a time been an exile in Sens.

The city museum at Sens is now located in what was once the bishop's palace, and its prize exhibit is the 'Sainte Châsse', an ivory casket probably brought (or looted) from Byzantium by Crusaders. Other church treasures now on display include a reliquary containing one of the many purported fragments of the True Cross, as well as a chalice made in England in the twelfth century and presumed to have been deposited at Sens Cathedral at some time during the English occupation of Normandy. Henry may not have been much impressed by the cathedral's treasures, if he saw them, since most of these items either had not yet been acquired or were not displayed at the time of his stay. A possible exception would have been the fragment of the Crown of Thorns that had been donated to the cathedral by King Louis IX ('Saint' Louis) on his return from crusade; the English king was soon to see the 'real thing' in Paris. The museum also contains a wooden statue of St Louis, carrying the Crown of Thorns. Saint Louis had been very attached to Sens and had been married in the cathedral. Henry is known to have revered the royal saint as representative of a 'golden age' of France which he intended to emulate when he became ruler of the kingdom.

After the fall of Sens, Henry returned his bride to her father's court at Troyes while he laid siege to Melun. As queen consort of England, Catherine acquired a bevy of female attendants, hand-picked and shipped to France to arrive shortly after the wedding. They included Thomas of Lancaster's wife, Margaret (previously the widow of one of Henry's Beaufort half-uncles) and Lady Margaret Mowbray, the sister of the Duke of Norfolk. Their arrival was delayed by the siege activity, and they did not meet their new queen until July. On the first of that month, Henry took Montereau, the site of the river crossing where John the Fearless had been killed less than a year earlier. His new ally, Philip the Good, was able to enter the defeated town and retrieve his father's body for re-burial at Dijon, the capital of Burgundy. The town's castle was slow to surrender, which resulted in Henry carrying out his threat to execute some of the prisoners he had taken in the town; the delay helped no one.

Montereau's old town, the 'ville basse', is on the southern bank of the River Yonne, close to its confluence with the Seine. Both rivers are crossed by several road bridges; the modern replacement for the medieval bridge on which John the Fearless was killed bears a plaque commemorating the event. Medieval illustrations show the castle keep in the background but this has long since disappeared. Nearby, the town's main place of worship, the 'Collégiale Notre-Dame-et-Saint-Loup de Montereau-Fault-Yonne', to give it its full name, is a medieval building completed over several centuries. This church, founded by an earlier Archbishop of Sens, is where John was given a temporary burial, along with his faithful lieutenant, Archambaud de Foix, and this is where Henry accompanied Philip the Good to retrieve the bodies and return them to Burgundy. The church still holds a sword claimed to have been John's, but certainly of too late a date.

Philip now worked in conjunction with Henry and his brother Bedford to take Melun. Soon they were joined by John 'the Pitiless', the new Duke of Bavaria, an ex-bishop who had recently snatched the duchy from his niece. True to his reputation, John urged Henry to make a hasty assault, but Henry recognised that the time had not yet arrived. He nevertheless allowed Philip and John to attack, with results that may have made them feel less cocky. While the siege was still proceeding, Henry began to miss his wife, and arranged for Catherine and her ladies to be housed in accommodation nearby. It must have been hard for them to tolerate the violence going on around them, and one of them, Margaret Mowbray, took solace in the arms of a relatively humble man-at-arms, Robert Howard; their son would one day inherit her brother's dukedom of Norfolk.

When Catherine's brother, the Dauphin, arrived with reinforcements in the hope of relieving the siege of Melun, he was unable to access the town because of the effective defences Henry had laid against him. A large new cannon, 'The London', was delivered to the king, a gift from the people of London which must have caused some consternation when seen by the defenders of Melun. The approaching winter made an impact on both besiegers and besieged, but on 18 November, after more than three months, Melun surrendered. Once again Henry proved ruthless in victory, allegedly leaving most of his prisoners to starve to death in the dungeons of various castles or in a ditch outside the town walls.

Melun's Norman Collégiale Notre-Dame, founded by the Capetian kings of France, became more widely known as the place of origin of the 'Melun Diptych', a devotional work created several decades after Henry's visit. The church Henry would have seen was, however, substantially the same as what stands today. It is located on the Île Saint-Etienne, in the oldest part of the town, but there are few other surviving remains of the medieval period, with the exception of the Priory of Saint-Sauveur. The Maison de la Vicomté, which houses the Musée de Melun, is a mainly nineteenth-century building.

Henry's immediate destination after accepting the surrender of Melun was Corbeil (Corbeil-Essonnes), midway to Paris, where he had another opportunity to spend a little time with his wife and his new in-laws before the festive season began. For once Henry did not need to size up the town's defences before entering. The remains of the medieval ramparts can still be seen, as can the Church (now cathedral) of St Spire, much altered over the centuries, which owes its fortifications to the fact that it lay outside the original town walls.

*****

On the first day of December, the French king and queen were able to return to Paris, escorted by their new son-in-law. This was surely one of the high points of Henry's whole reign. The Parisians dressed in red, the colour of celebration, to welcome the royals and their entourage. The weather was cold and the local economy had not yet recovered from the effects of the war. It has been suggested that Henry's popularity with the people of Paris did not last very long. Calling a parliament to approve the Treaty of Troyes was a sensible move, but he was also obliged to impose punitive measures to stabilise the economy and standardise the currency, including the reintroduction of the hated tax on salt known as the 'gabelle'. The city that had been growing so fast would become significantly depopulated after Henry's departure.

Immediately before Christmas, Henry joined his father-in-law at the Hotel St Pol to sit in judgment on the absent Dauphin. The new

Duke of Burgundy was demanding justice for his late father, and the Dauphin was called on to explain his role in the murder of John the Fearless. When he failed to turn up, he was officially banished from the kingdom and removed from the line of succession to the throne.

The ancient monuments of Paris suffered considerable damage during the French Revolution, but parts of the city contain enough medieval remains to give the visitor some idea of what it may have looked like in 1420, when Henry made his triumphant entry. Most people will be familiar with the cathedral of Notre-Dame de Paris, in the heart of the old city, which had been recognised as one of the French capital's most important buildings almost a hundred years before 1420, with Jean de Jandun (1285–1328) saying that it shone 'like the sun among stars'. Ten years later, Henry V's son would be crowned there.

The spire that was destroyed by the disastrous fire of April 2019 was not the medieval original, which had been taken down in the eighteeenth century and replaced by a grander structure. Even the sixteen statues, made of copper, that were saved because they had been removed before the fire broke out, date only from the nineteenth century. Thus the cathedral's exterior, with its distinctive twin towers, remains much as it would have appeared when Henry saw it, except that, like most medieval cathedrals in England as well as France, the façade would have been colourfully painted and gilded. The purpose of the statues of saints and illustrations of the Last Judgment was to remind the common people – a majority of whom were illiterate – of what the Bible taught and what might lie in store for them after death, depending on how well they behaved themselves.

When Notre Dame is fully rebuilt, at a cost currently estimated at $8 billion, it will not be in an updated style. The sections that were destroyed – the roof, the spire, and sections of the vaulting – will be modelled as closely as possible on the way the cathedral looked prior to the fire. Medieval techniques have been adopted to ensure that the stonework and woodwork match the original, the details of which were digitally recorded not long before the damage took place. The organ, the stained glass and the interior walls were all seriously damaged either by the fire or the measures taken to put it out, but all are able to be repaired rather than needing to be replaced. Thus, although it may be years before visitors are able to view the medieval building in its full glory, the restored cathedral will doubtless be as magnificent a sight as it was the day King Henry V entered Paris and saw it for the first time.

Beyond Notre-Dame lay the 'cloister', which contained living accommodation for the canons, the members of the cathedral chapter. Its original form is unknown, and its location is apparent only from the street names: the Rue Chanoinesse and Rue du Cloître Notre-Dame. This community was mainly occupied with giving boys a basic education. The eleventh-century scholar Peter Abelard had been a teacher here, and many of the church's highest dignitaries had learned how to read and write and received their early religious instruction here. Its entrance, at the end of the north transept, is marked by a statue of the Virgin Mary. This is far from unique: there are more than thirty statues of the Virgin (Notre Dame meaning 'Our Lady') within the cathedral precinct. The one that stands on a pedestal close to the altar is of an age with the building, but was brought here from the Chapelle Saint-Aignan, located in the east of the Île de la Cité, near the cathedral, after the original medieval statue was destroyed during the Revolution. Saint-Aignan is reputed to have been a meeting place for Abelard and his illicit lover Héloise. The few remains of the original chapel are now hidden behind an anonymous street frontage.

A few streets away, a plaque marks the supposed location of the house of Héloise's uncle, where the couple first became acquainted. It has been called 'the oldest house in Paris', but that accolade officially belongs to 51 rue de Montmorency, built in 1407 for the alchemist Nicolas Flamel (died 1418). Showing their age more obviously are numbers 11 and 13 rue François Miron, adjoining half-timbered houses, which have undergone considerable restoration in order to make them appear as they might have done in 1420, though all three houses are far enough away from the city centre not to have been on Henry's route.

Though the events had taken place 300 years earlier, the story of Abelard and Héloïse would have been well-known to the English king and the more literate members of his retinue. After their deaths, the couple's bones were supposedly buried together at the oratory in Ferreux-Quincey; in the nineteenth century they were brought to Père Lachaise Cemetery in Paris, where a monument can be seen. The popular French courtly poem, the thirteenth-century *Roman de la Rose*, was one of the first works to recount the story, which was later taken up by Chaucer and others. We may speculate on Henry's feelings about it; given his religious orthodoxy, he is unlikely to have approved of a love affair between a priest and a nun.

In addition to frequenting Notre-Dame, the would-be King of France would have been eager to view the holy relics brought back from crusade by St Louis: the Crown of Thorns and fragments of the true cross. His piety was such that his belief in the genuineness of these items would have been complete. Although temporarily housed at Notre-Dame when they were first brought back from the Holy Land, the relics were by 1420 held within a building that had been constructed for that specific purpose – the Sainte-Chapelle, built in the Gothic 'Rayonnant' style. Louis had also owned the tip of the 'Holy Lance', which he purchased from the Emperor Baldwin II of Constantinople. Henry would presumably have been allowed to view the royal saint's own undershirt, first recorded in 1418 as being held in Charles VI's treasury. The garment, which may well be genuine, was eventually moved to Notre-Dame, and was saved from the 2019 fire along with the other relics.

After the Sainte-Chapelle was damaged during the Revolution, the relics were returned to Notre-Dame, where they were put on display in the cathedral treasury; the reliquaries survived only because their artistic merit was recognised by the authorities. Following the

2019 fire, they were temporarily placed in the Louvre. Like Notre-Dame, the Sainte-Chapelle has been significantly restored in the past 200 years, and the building we see today is very like what Henry would have seen. It was built on two levels, and originally had a ceremonial staircase by which the king could enter the royal chapel, on the upper level, directly from outside. The lower level was used as a parish church, not for the use of the general populace but for those who lived within the palace complex.

The Sainte-Chapelle was situated within the Palais de la Cité, a royal palace that was rebuilt many times. It stood on the central 'Île de la Cité', at the north-western end of the island, the opposite end from Notre-Dame, on the site now occupied by the Palais de Justice. King Charles V ceased to use it as a palace after the 1350s, and the only medieval survival is the 'Conciergerie', nowadays occupied mainly by law courts. During the revolutionary period, it was used as a prison. Parts of the building are open to the public, but the pseudo-medieval exterior is deceptive. Inside, however, the great hall has been largely preserved under the name 'La Salle des Gens d'Armes' (The Hall of the Soldiers), as has the smaller 'Salle des Gardes'.

The Île de la Cité was well-equipped with churches, almost none of which survive. Elsewhere in the city, there remain few medieval churches, thanks mainly to the revolutionary fervour of the late eighteenth century, in the course of which so many were damaged or destroyed. The Hôtel-Dieu, possibly the world's oldest hospital, was founded in the seventh century, and was significantly extended over the centuries, with an ethos of never turning away a sick person. The original building has long since been replaced, but it still occupies the same site on the Île de la Cité. The Tour Saint-Jacques, a prominent landmark that looks across at the Conciergerie from the right bank of the Seine, is all that is left of the church of Saint-Jacques-de-la-Boucherie; although built in the Flamboyant Gothic style, it was not begun until 1509.

One of the finest medieval churches still standing in Paris is Saint-Eustache, located in Les Halles, the food market in the north of the city. It dates to the thirteenth century, but the church that now bears the name is much bigger and more elaborate, as a result of a sixteenth-century rebuild, and is far removed in both external and internal appearance from the church of 1420. Its star exhibits were the relics of St Eustache, donated by the Abbey of St Denis. In complete contrast, the church of Saint-Julien-le-Pauvre, on the Left Bank, is one of the oldest churches in Paris and much of its medieval appearance has been preserved, albeit with some confusing and anachronistic architectural features. It dates to the twelfth century, and was built by the Cluniac order to provide shelter for pilgrims. It was never completed, and the seventeenth-century reconstruction, coupled with a nineteenth-century restoration project, resulted in a complete change of the overall design. Thankfully, it escaped a scheduled demolition and it now belongs to the Melkite-Greek Catholic denomination.

Outside the city walls, the Basilica of Saint-Denis, where Henry had previously stopped to pray, was a place of pilgrimage originally built over the site of a Gallo-Roman cemetery. Bishop Denis, the martyr it commemorates, was beheaded in around the year 250 and would later be adopted as the patron saint, not just of Paris but of the whole country of France. He was said to be buried at the basilica, but the canons of Notre-Dame disputed this, claiming that they possessed a section of his skull at their cathedral. The king's battle standard, the *oriflamme*, was blessed at Saint-Denis and had been held there since it was last used at Agincourt. With these sacred and royal connections, the basilica must have been an inspiration to Henry, though he never aspired to be buried there himself. As it appears today, the church lacks its north tower, which was removed following storm damage in the mid-nineteenth century; a twenty-first-century project to reconstruct it is at the planning stage. The Valois chapel was a later addition, and the Valois kings of the fifteenth century, including Charles VI, are buried in the main part of the basilica with their ancestors. Their tombs were damaged, and some of the bodies removed, during the French Revolution, so that the effigies seen now are empty representations of a few bones that lie in the ossuary.

The city of Paris had grown so fast that King Charles V had been obliged to build new walls on the Right Bank, to replace those constructed 200 years earlier by Philip II for the same reason. Fragments of Philip's wall can still be seen in a historic quarter of the city, close to the much later church of St Paul and St Louis. Charles's additions included the fortress known as the Bastille, later notorious as a prison. Its original purpose was to protect the main eastern entrance to the city, the Porte Saint-Antoine. It was by this route that any English attack was anticipated. It was Charles VI's government that had begun using it as a prison, in 1417, and its ditches, bastions and eight massive towers must have been a fearful sight for new inmates. The Dauphin Charles had even taken refuge there when the Duke of Burgundy seized Paris in 1418. With the towers all at the same height, the Bastille was made to a very different, and much stronger, design than the traditional French castle, and it was copied at several other locations. Nunney Castle in Somerset, England, although built as a small private residence, gives the visitor some idea of how startling this new architectural trend would have been to those familiar with the standard Norman castle.

With the construction of the new walls, the fortress known as the Grand Châtelet, which was located on the site of the present Place du Châtelet on the Right Bank of the Seine, no longer fulfilled its original defensive function, and was converted to a law court and prison. Charles V had rebuilt it, but within a few years of the death of Henry V it had fallen out of use and the magistrates' court was moved to the Louvre. Although the Grand Châtelet was later rebuilt, it was demolished early in the nineteenth century. There was also a Petit Châtelet, which stood by the Petit Pont that still links the Île de la Cité to the Right Bank. In 1408, the bridge was swept away, and it had only recently been rebuilt when Henry arrived. This was not the last time such an event took place, and the present Petit Pont dates from the nineteenth century. The Petit Châtelet was demolished in the 1790s.

There was of course also a Grand Pont, probably constructed in Roman times, on the Left Bank, on the site where the Pont Notre-Dame now stands. Like its smaller equivalent on the other side of the Île de la Cité, it had been washed away by floods and rebuilt on several occasions. Most recently, it had been re-erected by Charles VI, in wood, in 1412 and it was at this time that it was re-named the Pont Notre-Dame, perhaps in hopes that dedicating it to Our Lady would protect it from further destruction. Eventually, the weight of the wooden houses constructed on it would contribute to its collapse, but at the time of Henry's arrival, it was brand new and had been dubbed by a contemporary 'the handsomest in France'.[4] Until the Pont-Neuf was built in the last sixteenth century, these two bridges were the only real option for those needing to cross the Seine in Paris without travelling on water.

There was a second large island in the Seine, the Île Saint-Louis, but this remained undeveloped until the seventeenth century. Nevertheless, Paris was a crowded and bustling city, in the same way as London and other large European cities. Any spare land on the banks of the Seine was taken up by daily markets, and the larger bridges were lined with shops and houses. As we have seen, the number of bridges available for public use was small, whilst the river was considerably wider than it is now, making them more difficult to build. Since the crossing of a river bridge typically required the payment of a toll, the ferry trade was healthy, with boats large and small plying to and fro incessantly. Following the siege of Melun, many prisoners had been shipped to Paris by the Seine, and had been incarcerated in several of the available fortresses: the Bastille, the prison in the palace complex, and the Grand Châtelet. Those

---

4. Robert Gauguin.

consigned to the latter are reputed to have been deliberately starved to death while their captors mocked them.

The left bank of the Seine was largely occupied by monastic establishments at this period. Chief among these was the ancient Abbey of Saint-Germain-des-Prés, founded by the Frankish kings in the sixth century. This abbey owned and administered most of the land in the district, as well as some outside the city walls. The Saint-Germain quarter of Paris, also known as the 'Latin Quarter' because of its international student population who were obliged to use Latin for everyday communication, grew up around it, with a reputation as a centre of learning and culture which it retains. The monastery lost its status after the French Revolution, but the abbey church, with its eleventh-century Norman tower, survives. In the early fifteenth century, the abbey also housed an important scriptorium and library, which was destroyed by fire during the revolution.

Whereas Charles VI and Queen Isabeau resided at the Hotel St Pol with a small court, 'poorly and meanly attended',[5] Henry and his retinue enjoyed the relative grandeur of the Louvre. Charles VI actually preferred the Hotel St Pol over the Louvre for its more intimate atmosphere. This was despite his experience of 1493, when he had danced there in a group of six men at a masked ball (the 'Bal des Ardents') and was one of only two to survive the fire that broke out; he escaped injury thanks to a conveniently-located duchess who threw her skirt over him to put out the flames. Yet there were happier memories too: his daughter Catherine had been born and brought up in these surroundings. Charles valued his privacy and it was no hardship for the royal family to stay at this quieter residence.

The Hotel St Pol was located on the north bank of the Seine, in the vicinity of the Porte St Antoine and the Bastille, but there are no remains to be seen today. It had been created by Catherine's

---

5. Monstrelet

Second French Campaign – Rouen and Paris

grandfather, King Charles V, from several earlier public buildings (called 'hotels', but with a different meaning from the English word). In general, the French royal family had concentrated on building and renewing properties in their traditional home territory of Paris and the Loire valley. They had taken a limited interest in Normandy, which had been in and out of their hands during the 350 years since William the Conqueror invaded England. Within a hundred years, the Hotel St Pol would be disused and derelict and it was demolished in the sixteenth century.

During his brief ascendancy, John the Fearless had made use of another building in Paris, of which one wing survives. The 'Tour Jean-sans-Peur', as it is now known, stands back from the road, in the Rue Etienne-Morel, looking extremely out of place among the busy shoppers and café-goers. This defensive structure was part of a much bigger, L-shaped building, sometimes called the Hôtel de Bourgogne, incorporated into the city walls. Originally constructed in the thirteenth century, it had been acquired by the Dukes of Burgundy in about 1370, but the tower was added in about 1410 at John's behest. Five storeys tall, it protected the occupants against attack (despite his nickname, John was rightly fearful of assassination) by having no access from the ground to the first floor. A grand staircase led up to the living quarters, resembling the arrangement within the Louvre. The most prominent aspect of the décor is the carved stone ceiling at the top of the stair, adorned with plants that were emblems of the Burgundy family - the oak tree, the hawthorn and the hop. The original floor tiles, some of which have been rediscovered during archaeological excavations, were decorated with marguerites, the emblem of John's mother.

Henry's temporary residence following his marriage was not the Louvre as we know it now, but a castle that stood on the same site until the mid-sixteenth century. It was a square structure, with ten defensive towers, close to the River Seine, from which it drew the water for its moat. The main entrance faced south, towards the river.

Although built as a strong fortress, the Louvre had been converted by King Louis IX to a royal residence and extended further by King Charles V. After 1420, when Henry moved into Paris, the French royal family preferred their residences further south, and within a hundred years the Louvre had been mostly demolished by Charles VI's successors. It was a later king, Francis I, who turned it into the Renaissance building we are used to seeing, which covers around four times as big an area as the castle, much of which is taken up by the square courtyard at its heart.

English nobles flocked to Paris to share the Christmas festivities. These included Thomas's wife Margaret, and Philippa, Duchess of York, the widow of Henry's uncle Edward. It was reported that the courtiers dressed richly, with Henry habitually wearing a crown to remind everyone of his status. His love of music is well-attested and he took a band of musicians with him everywhere he went. Members of the Chapel Royal had been present at the Battle of Agincourt, to celebrate the victory in song, and the Dean of the Chapel Royal, John Gilbert, had been present during most of Henry's campaigns. The celebration of Christmas 1420 was probably the occasion when one of the earliest known English carols, 'Princeps Pacis' ('Prince of Peace') was performed for the first time.

French, as well as English, nobles congregated around Henry in hopes of currying favour, hence their neglect of the absent king of France. As for Charles, he had earned criticism for hosting a Christmas feast that was well below the accustomed standard. Despite the fact that some of the Parisians had been practically begging Henry to come and take over, replacing their mad king and his feeble son, the arrival of the English was now beginning to feel like an invasion by unwelcome foreigners intent on taking more than their fair share of France's worldly goods. Parisians were used to a rigid social structure, from which it was difficult for individuals to escape. A large percentage lived below the poverty line, but philanthropy was considered a responsibility of the wealthy, who no doubt felt their position threatened by the influx of so many foreigners.

Outside the palace, the population of Paris was starving. The recent war had taken its toll. The Burgundian chronicler Georges Chastellain, who was still a child at the time, writes that the conduct of the English was so arrogant and so dismissive of the French people that Henry quickly fell out of favour with his prospective subjects. It was said that he berated Jehan de Villers, Seigneur de l'Isle-Adam, for wearing shabby clothes and daring to look him in the face; this was hardly surprising, since Villers had been the leader of the Dauphin's garrison at Pontoise.

In the meantime, England's parliament was becoming impatient to see the king again, and sent an urgent message to this effect, to which he soon responded. By the time Henry and Catherine left for England, the king would have been out of the country for three years. He nevertheless paused to call a parliament at Rouen, where he arrived with his queen on 27 December. There the French, as well as approving the Treaty of Troyes, agreed to impose a new hearth tax on their own people. In January, Henry and Catherine set out for Calais, with a stopover at Amiens.

Return to England

It was early February before Henry and his new wife were back in his capital. The *Bedford Hours*, an illustrated manuscript made in France and once owned by Henry's son, King Henry VI, contains idealised images of the happy couple. After an ecstatic reception at Dover on the first of the month, Henry began making his way to London, no doubt preoccupied with the preparations for the coronation of his queen, who would follow in a few days. Just as had happened when Henry returned home in 1415, the couple received an enthusiastic welcome on arriving in Blackheath, on their way to the city. This was a traditional spot for the reception of royals and other dignitaries, and was where Henry himself had been greeted by the capital's bigwigs after his first successful campaign in France. Catherine was welcomed with another elaborate pageant, once again featuring figures of giants, apostles, virgins, and other characters supplied by the costumiers.

On the following day, 23 February, Catherine was escorted from the Tower of London to Westminster Abbey, where she was crowned queen by Archbishop Chichele. Henry was not present in the abbey, since it was not usual for the king to attend the coronation of a new consort. The queen was not short of attendants, however: Holinshed's *Chronicle* includes the rather startling detail that one of the queen's ladies, the Countess of Kent, sat *under* the table at the queen's feet, holding a napkin in readiness for her mistress's use. This would be the exotic Lucia Visconti, the daughter of the Duke of Milan and widow of one of the king's distant cousins.

In Henry's absence, there was still a reigning monarch in attendance at the coronation, in the form of King James I of Scotland, relations between him and Henry now being fully restored. At the coronation banquet, following the lavish ceremony, James was honoured by being placed at the queen's left hand. She obligingly made a formal request to her husband for the Scottish king to be freed; this would be publicly acknowledged by her husband, but privately and politely ignored.

Everything about the feast was imbued with symbolism. An image of St Catherine was displayed on the banqueting table. Since it was Lent, the first, second and third courses all consisted mainly of fish dishes, as well as a 'leche' or jelly decorated with the king's motto and a 'flampayne' or pie decorated with golden crowns and fleur-de-lis emblems. Another image of St Catherine turned up later in the meal, and the pièce de résistance was a model of a knight on horseback vanquishing a small tiger (apparently representing the Dauphin).

Despite the festivities, Henry soon abandoned his bride in London while he went on progress around the country, trying to raise money for his next expedition. Despite the imagery at the coronation feast, the Dauphin was not yet finally defeated (and never would be). Catherine would make her own separate tour of the country, her route not always coinciding with her husband's, but did not leave the capital until just over a week before Easter. Henry began in Bristol, showing his face to the south-west of England before going on to Coventry and then Leicester.

Catherine travelled north via Hertford, Bedford and Northampton, arriving the day before Palm Sunday at Henry's old home, Leicester Castle, where the couple were reunited for Easter. Perhaps this was when the young queen took delivery of a harp Henry had ordered for her the previous autumn. He had ordered a new one for himself as well, possibly with the intention of them enjoying playing together. Clearly, they were not averse to one another's company, because, by the time Henry left on another business trip, Catherine was pregnant.

Nottingham, Pontefract and York were the king's next ports of call, Catherine accompanying him only as far as Pontefract. Henry saw his journey around England partly as a pilgrimage, and one of his destinations after parting company with his wife was the shrine of St John at Beverley, where he was accompanied by King James. Beverley Minster is a huge Gothic church, whose two imposing towers had been constructed only a few years before Henry made his first visit there as Prince of Wales, and must have impressed him greatly. The shrine of St John had been rebuilt about a hundred years earlier, but this was dismantled following the Reformation. However, shortly after Henry became king, a local worthy would donate the money for a new east window, which was restored after being damaged during the Reformation and can still be seen by visitors. Bridlington Priory, which Henry had also visited on his pilgrimage to Yorkshire while Prince of Wales, fared less well in later years, and its shrine to John Twenge has disappeared. The remains of the priory church – the nave and the gatehouse – are incorporated into the parish church of St Mary, which was rebuilt in the nineteenth century.

The tomb of St John of Beverley had reportedly been the location of a minor miracle just as the king was winning the Battle of Agincourt, and he would have been praying for the saint's continued support in his next campaign. It was while in the north that he received some devastating news from France, which must have made him even more determined to subdue the remaining opposition to his rule, but would also have given him pause for thought about his place in God's favour.

Almost as soon as Henry and Catherine left France, the Dauphin Charles had renewed his efforts to win back his birthright. While the newly-weds were enjoying the Easter holiday together, Henry would not have known that his brother, Thomas, whom he had left to command his armies in Normandy when he brought Catherine home at the beginning of the year, was planning a rash surprise attack on a large French army led jointly by Marshal La Fayette and a Scottish commander, the Earl of Buchan, at Baugé, near Angers. Ignoring the advice of veteran commanders like the Earl of Huntingdon, Thomas made the classic error of splitting his forces, leaving his army outnumbered. Perhaps he fancied his chances of carrying off another Agincourt, but the English force was routed and Thomas himself was killed. Several other English noblemen lost their lives in the attack, including the Agincourt veteran John Grey, Earl of Tankerville. Huntingdon was taken prisoner and would not be released for nearly four years. The captured English standard was delivered to the Dauphin, and the faithful Salisbury was left to pick up the pieces.

After parting from the king, Catherine made her own progress around England, supporting Henry's cause, while he took a different route, calling in at Lincoln, Lynn (now King's Lynn), Walsingham – the location of another major holy shrine – and Norwich, to drum up support for a third French campaign. Although he is said to have taken the news of Thomas's death with his usual composure, it meant that campaigning once again rose to the top of his agenda. The young queen gamely carried on without him, visiting towns and cities in the east of England: Stamford, Huntingdon, Cambridge and Colchester.

By the time she began preparing for her confinement at Windsor, the king was off again on his travels.

Henry had to return to London at the beginning of May for the parliament he had already called; despite all his gains, he had overspent and needed the money, as well as wanting to ratify the Treaty of Troyes. To ensure the latter, he had to address Parliament's concerns about the possibility of his introducing French laws into England. The opposite was always more likely, though Henry would attempt to rule Normandy in much the same manner as his forefathers had done, and he obtained everything he wanted. While he was about it, he addressed a crowd of 360 Benedictines, lecturing them on their religious responsibilities. Henry Beaufort was the leading light among the churchmen who rallied round to offer financial assistance, ensuring that there was no need for wrangling with parliament. Beaufort had an ulterior motive; he was temporarily in the king's bad books after having been offered a cardinal's hat by the new pope.

The business did not take long to complete, and the king was soon ready to depart. By the early summer, Henry would have been aware that Catherine was pregnant. Although she eventually followed him to France, she would not see him in the final few weeks of his life, and Henry would never set eyes on the child she was carrying.

Chapter 8

France: The Final Campaign

At Dover, the king paused long enough to make a will. It was not the first time he had done such a thing before departing for war, but perhaps the death of his brother Thomas had reminded him of his own mortality. Despite their ups and downs, Henry and Thomas had worked as a team for many years, and it was a loss that would have hit the king hard. Thomas had been next in line for the throne, and the knowledge that the queen was pregnant made Henry realise that the kingdom needed to be prepared for the possibility of a regency. On 10 June 1421, he set out again for France after a stay of fewer than six months in his own kingdom, and reached Calais the same day. Despite Salisbury's written assurances that he could handle the situation, Henry could not wait to continue what he had started.

The vanguard of Henry's army set out for Paris, while the king himself headed for Montreuil, where he was to meet Duke Philip of Burgundy to discuss strategy. The Dauphin Charles had besieged the city of Chartres, the main city of the Beauce region, which had been in Burgundian hands since 1417, and relieving the siege was a matter of urgency. The news that the King of England was on his way, however, caused the Dauphin to retreat. Having stopped over briefly in Paris, Henry made for Dreux, one of the Dauphin's few strongholds, which he proceeded to besiege. The substantial French garrison had little appetite for resistance, and they surrendered within three weeks. The English arrived in Chartres to a rapturous reception from a garrison made up of their fellow countrymen and allies.

Chartres today is noted mainly for its cathedral, now a UNESCO World Heritage site, which had been completed two hundred years before Henry's arrival. It houses a holy relic, the 'Sancta Camisa', a robe said to have been worn by the Virgin Mary. This had been presented to the city by Charles the Bald way back in the ninth century, and since then had been credited with many miracles and had even survived a destructive fire in the late twelfth century. A man as religious as Henry V might well have believed that the Dauphin's retreat was yet another sign of the relic's miraculous powers, and would have revered it accordingly. Thought to have been destroyed during the French Revolution, part of the robe was later recovered and continues to be prominently displayed in the cathedral.

Although it met a number of calamities in the intervening centuries, Chartres Cathedral nowadays looks very similar to how it would have looked when Henry arrived in the city in 1421. This was largely thanks to Henry's hero, St Louis, who had overseen the reconstruction. Early in the next century, one of the spires was struck by lightning and rebuilt in a different style, but the most significant changes are to the interior. However, the 'labyrinth', which forms part of the cathedral floor and is therefore not always visible to visitors, is thought to date from the thirteenth century; it is an abstract depiction of the journey of a pilgrim. Much of the twelfth-century stained glass also survives, and adjacent to the cathedral, in the cathedral close, is the Centre International du Vitrail, comprising temporary and permanent exhibitions of stained glass as well as a training centre for contemporary stained glass artists.

The former bishop's palace, adjacent to the cathedral, is a much later building that now houses the city's Musée des Beaux-Arts. However, Chartres still contains a number of medieval churches and one or two houses of the period. Small sections of the city walls survive among the cobbled streets south of the cathedral; though Henry never needed to attack them, they were seriously damaged in later years, notably during the Second World War.

*****

The Dauphin Charles had now moved on to Beaugency, and this was Henry's next target. His troops moved swiftly to attack and take the town, but the castle held out for some time, making it difficult to use the bridge over the river Loire, even to parley with the enemy. The bridge, with its twenty-three arches, is as impressive now as it would have been in the fifteenth century, since it was completely rebuilt in 1946 after being destroyed during the Second World War. Meanwhile, Beaugency's massive eleventh-century keep retains its medieval appearance.

Henry had gone further south in the hope of a battle with the Dauphin, but that strategy failed. Eluded by the enemy's army, Henry changed tactic and decided to attack the Dauphin's other territories in the region. He was hampered by an outbreak of disease among his own men, which made it impossible for him to attempt the capture of Orléans. At length, Henry ensconced himself at Nemours, where the strong castle (now a museum) would have seemed suitable accommodation for a king. Overlooking the River Loing, the city had long been the centre of a royal duchy, but the castle was not the elegant palace it appears today, since it would be significantly improved by its owners in the course of the next hundred years. Significant renovations were carried out in the years 2005-8, offering visitors an enhanced experience.

Many of the city's buildings had been burned down during the wars with Edward III. The rebuilding of the church of Saint-Jean-Baptiste did not begin until the 1440s, so the church we see next to the castle today, although medieval in origin, is substantially different from the ruinous condition in which Henry found it. Around the castle courtyard, however, several medieval buildings have survived, giving visitors the opportunity to walk along cobbled lanes and imbibe some of the atmosphere of the fifteenth century.

In September, the English made quick work of besieging Rougement, a well-fortified settlement where the Dauphin's supporters had been taking refuge within easy reach of Paris. After taking the town, Henry burned it to the ground, and allegedly threw any survivors into the river, thus enhancing his reputation for ruthlessness. The nearby town of Montargis surrendered quickly when they heard the English were on their way. Henry had been back in France for four months when he made the fateful decision to lay siege to Meaux.

After keeping Christmas with the French king and queen, Henry returned to the campaign trail. Meaux was the most strategically important of the Dauphin's remaining strongholds, and it was vital for the English to take it if they were to maintain supremacy. The former Earl of Dorset, now Duke of Exeter, was sent ahead to assert control of the outlying areas, but the city itself was a daunting prospect. The English had taken stronger fortresses, but it seems from contemporary documents that Henry's resources were stretched and he was a little short of manpower. Meaux's location, on a bend of the river Marne, made it particularly well-protected, and the occupants were well-provided with artillery and other weapons. Once again, the king chose the nearest religious house, the abbey of Saint Faro(n), for his place of residence during the siege. This was destroyed during the French Revolution. The abbot of Saint Faro, Philippe de Gamaches, was no fan of the English, and was already inside the city fighting for the defenders, along with some of the monks. It happened that Philippe's brother, Guillaume de Gamaches, was responsible for the defence of Compiègne, and volunteered to give up that city in exchange for Philippe's life being spared.

Meaux's old city walls have partly survived. Originally constructed by the Romans in the third century AD to protect against possible barbarian invasion, they were strengthened and extended in the 200 years or so before Henry's arrival, with round defensive towers being added at intervals. Some of these can still be seen, and the remains of the walls can be viewed to advantage from the Bossuet garden, a seventeenth-century formal garden on the site of what would have been the residence of the Bishop of Meaux at the time of the siege.

After constructing the usual palisades and earthworks around the city, the English began their bombardment of the walls. Although they at first had some success, the casualties began to pile up in the course of the siege, including the 7th Lord Clifford, and John Cornwall, seventeen-year-old son and heir of Lord Fanhope, a veteran of Agincourt; Fanhope was unfortunate enough to witness his son's death, and swore never to fight again. Richard Beauchamp, the young Earl of Worcester, who had been awarded the earldom only a year before, was also killed by cannon fire from the city. It took considerable effort to make an impact on the defences, and winter was closing in. In December, the Marne, always highly prone to winter flooding, burst its banks and destroyed Henry's pontoon bridge. The English had to leave some of their forward positions, and the waterlogged conditions began to be reminiscent of the siege of Harfleur.

Whereas normally everything the king touched turned to gold, he seemed to be fighting an uphill battle, as the enemy kept finding ways around the attackers, threatening their supply lines and forcing them to divide their already thinly-stretched human resources still further. Henry wrote to seek assistance from Louis, the Elector Palatine, the husband of the king's late sister Blanche, who had died before Henry came to the throne. At around this time another outbreak of sickness began among the troops. Men were falling ill of dysentery or were victims of an outbreak of smallpox. It was a long and bitter campaign, lasting seven months. Henry's chief opponent was the so-called 'Bastard of Vaurus"' a man with a widespread reputation for savagery, who was summarily executed at the end of the siege. By December 1421, when news arrived of the birth of a son and heir back home at Windsor, the king was already ill, but he refused to leave until the city was taken.

At one point, the inhabitants of Meaux are said to have had a donkey brought up onto the walls, and likened the noise it made to the sound of the English king's voice. Perhaps they had heard a lot of this while Henry was shouting orders at the besiegers as he directed operations. As the siege dragged on, however, Henry's illness may have kept him indoors more than usual. He remained at the abbey of Saint Faro(n) de Meaux. One of the most revered names in the city was that of Saint Fiacre, a seventh-century Irish monk who had been a resident of the abbey and had left a shrine there. Some began to believe that Henry's attack on Meaux had called down the saint's wrath, and that this was the true cause of his illness. Perhaps the king himself was beginning to wonder. His belief in himself as God's chosen instrument had been an important factor in his successes up to now, and any creeping doubts in this respect may have affected him adversely.

In March, some of the Dauphin's supporters, led by Guy de Nesle, attempted to enter the city to support the resistance effort, but he was captured by the English and this damaged the morale of the garrison, who left their posts to take refuge in the city market, allowing the enemy to enter. A portable tower was brought in to deal with the remaining opposition. Richard Beauchamp, cousin and namesake of the Earl of Warwick, had been created Earl of Worcester only a year earlier; he was killed in the attack on the market, losing Henry another reliable supporter. Eager for vengeance, Warwick did not take long to break down the remaining defences, while Sir Walter Hungerford, an experienced siege commander, successfully bridged the river and mined the walls. The people of Meaux eventually surrendered in May 1422, and on the tenth of that month, the English king took possession of the city. He spared the lives of the occupants, with the exception of some Scottish, Irish and English adversaries whose loyalty had been found wanting. (The young Scottish king, still nominally Henry's prisoner, was present in person at the siege, in support of the English.)

Henry was now able to help himself to substantial supplies of food, weapons and other useful items, and was finally free to return to Paris. Following the baptism of the future King Henry VI in England, with the king's brother, the Duke of Bedford, as one of his godparents, Catherine had written to her husband, asking to be allowed to join him in France. She was not allowed to do so until May, when she crossed to Harfleur and they met in Paris. Leaving the baby with a wet-nurse, under the protection of Humphrey of Gloucester, Catherine had been escorted to the agreed meeting place by Bedford, and was patiently awaiting a reunion. She must surely have been a little shocked at seeing her husband so thin, ill and worn out.

Charles VI and Queen Isabeau arrived in Paris where they took up their lodgings at the Hotel St Pol as usual, whilst Catherine was received at the Louvre. In June 1422, Henry and Catherine celebrated Whitsun with a 'marvellously glorious' feast. The Parisians put on a mystery play, based on the story of St George, in order to honour the couple, but some accounts claim that they were disappointed with the lack of hospitality shown by the English. The weather was oppressively hot, disease was rife, and the royal family soon moved their court to Senlis. In Henry's weakened state, he was vulnerable to additional infections, and his condition grew worse instead of better. The doctors were failing him, and a more trusted physician was summoned from England.

The royal palace at Senlis, although now in ruins, is comparatively well-preserved. It was completed in the twelfth century and was constructed so as to take advantage of the protection offered by the city walls, themselves originally built by the Romans. Still visible are the remains of the great hall, the treasury, the bedchambers, the chapel and the domestic quarters. There are few better places one could go to enjoy the atmosphere of the times, since the city of Senlis retains its medieval shape and charm, its meandering cobbled alleyways strewn with quaint, higgledy-piggledy houses. The cathedral, despite later alterations, is unmistakably Gothic in style, whilst the Norman origins of the church of the former Abbey of St Vincent are also clear.

Although Henry was far from recovered, he was off again within weeks, leaving Catherine behind at Senlis. While the King of England was busy making deals with the Duke of Burgundy and planning his next move, the Dauphin made a surprise attack on Nevers in Burgundy. Duke Philip immediately deserted Henry and set out to confront the Dauphin, accompanied by some of the English archers. In the meantime, the king became too weak to ride, and the party got as far as Corbeil, where they paused to allow Henry to rest. While staying there, he signed official papers, showing that he still imagined himself in control of the country. He was headed south, but after a time his poor state of health forced him to travel in a litter.

Early in August the English met up with their Burgundian allies at Cosne, where they expected to hold a pitched battle with the Dauphin. The Dauphin and his allies had left in a hurry when they heard that the English and Burgundian forces were on their way. Duke Philip retreated to Bourges, whilst Henry was moved to Vincennes, where he died at the age of thirty-five. At the time, some believed his illness to be smallpox, of which there had been a recent outbreak in Paris. More recently, some have suggested that heatstroke was a contributory factor. There was even talk of leprosy, but historians generally accept that cause of death was the dysentery that he had contracted during the siege of Meaux. Present at his bedside were his brother, Bedford, and his old friend the Earl of Warwick. Historians generally agree that his wife Catherine was still at Senlis and not with the royal entourage.

*****

The Chateau de Vincennes, now a popular tourist destination, was originally constructed during the twelfth century, for the French king, Louis VII, and was enlarged during the following hundred years by two of his successors. However, the *donjon* tower, where Henry ended his life, was a relatively new building, unusually tall even for a fortification at 50 metres, exceeded in height only by the tower at Coucy. It was one of the French royal family's official residences, and King Charles V, so much more effectual a monarch than his unstable son, had been born there and had kept part of his enormous library there. The Chateau de Vincennes was more than a castle, it was a small town.

Perhaps it was to Charles V's former bedchamber on the first floor that Henry was taken when he was no longer strong enough to carry on his normal activities. On arrival, he would have taken little notice of the castle's grandeur, if he was even conscious. For months he had tried to deny his illness, but by now he must have been aware that he was dying. The best he might have hoped for at this stage was to live long enough to see his infant son again and perhaps help guide him on the path to kingship. It was not to be. On 26 August, a few days before his death, the king added codicils to his will to ensure that his debts were paid. His thoughts also turned to his stepmother, Joanna of Navarre, who had been falsely accused of witchcraft in 1419, while he was out of the country. As long as the matter remained unresolved, he had been ready enough to appropriate some of her income, but now he ordered that she be released from her confinement and receive financial restitution.

Henry died in the early hours of the morning on 31 August 1422, having reigned for less than ten years. The chronicler Walsingham wrote that 'he did not leave his like on earth among Christian kings and princes, so that not only the people of England and France but all Christendom mourned his death…'. Clearly, this is not true. Charles VI, himself only two months away from death, may have had ambivalent feelings on hearing that Henry was gone. The Dauphin Charles must surely have celebrated when the news reached him, as no doubt did most of 'free' France. There must have been some Frenchmen, however, whose feelings were less optimistic on seeing the prospect of living in peace under a strong and sane ruler snatched away from them.

By the time of Henry's death, he had been suffering for so long that his body had wasted away to almost nothing. It was transported to Saint Denis, for embalming, but did not enter Paris on its way to Rouen, where it again lay in state. Catherine travelled with the cortege, but she and her retinue remained a long distance behind the coffin, which was accompanied by her husband's most trusted supporters, including the Duke of Exeter, the Earl of March, and Sir Lewis Robessart. They finally arrived in Calais on 12 October, and eventually crossed to Dover on 31 October.

The king's body was being returned to England for burial at Westminster Abbey, where he had arranged for a chantry chapel. On 5 November, the aldermen and other most important officials of London, dressed in black, headed a torchlight procession to St George's Bar, and hence to St Paul's. Next day, the coffin was drawn in a chariot pulled by four horses right into the nave of Westminster Abbey, with a painted effigy, made from boiled leather, disguising the condition of the corpse. The construction of the chantry, of Caen stone, was completed in 1450.

Henry's tomb was opened during the 1950s and it was discovered that another body was also present, that of Bishop Richard Courtenay, who had died at Harfleur while serving the king. The likely explanation is that Courtenay's burial was accidentally disturbed when Henry's tomb was built. Henry's effigy is not the original one, of Purbeck marble, but was partially recreated in 1971 out of resin to replace the silver decoration that originally adorned the carved figure; the silver was stolen sometime in the sixteenth century, shortly after the Reformation. Henry's effigy shows the king wearing a crown and in long robes, not the armour one might have expected. Originally the effigy also held two sceptres, and angels stood at the head, with lions lying at his feet; all these are now missing.

A shield, saddle and helmet, the 'achievements' that were normally displayed on a warrior's tomb, are now to be found in the Queen's Diamond Jubilee Galleries, located in the medieval triforium at the Abbey. The helmet, which is dented, is almost certainly not genuinely Henry's, but it may have been this dent that gave rise to the legend that the king was targeted at the height of the Battle of Agincourt by a large group of French knights, one of whom got close enough to strike a blow. As for the shield, that is thought to have belonged to his father. Likewise, the sword that is also on display has no provenance;

from its style, experts believe it to have been manufactured in the middle of the 15th century and thus too late to have been Henry's.

An inscription on the tomb reads: 'Henry V, hammer of the Gauls, lies here. Henry was put in the urn 1422. Virtue conquers all. The fair Catherine finally joined her husband 1437. Flee idleness.' Catherine is not, however, buried with her husband. Her remains were laid to rest in the Lady Chapel and later moved closer to Henry's by her grandson King Henry VII, eventually ending up under the altar in the chantry.

Conclusion

The English had never had a king quite like Henry V; he retains an almost impeccable reputation not shared by any other king of England. True, England had one of the greatest warrior kings of all time in Richard I, 200 years earlier, but Richard had never shown any interest in governing England and had spent more time out of the country than in it. The closest thing to Henry the English monarchy had to offer was Edward III, who had also shown signs of great future promise as a teenager, promise that had come to fruition in adulthood when he assumed the throne and a new regime hit the ground running. Unlike Edward III, Henry remained unmarried until his thirties and thus represented a myriad of possible advantageous alliances with other nations. Although he had not planned to remain single, the benefits became apparent as he looked for ways to secure his claim to the French throne. Unlike Edward III, he did not assault the virtue of his courtiers' wives. The disadvantages of his delay in marrying would become apparent only when he contracted his final sickness, leaving a small child to inherit the throne. If Henry V was another Edward III, Henry VI was likewise another Richard II.

Within a few years of his death, Henry's youngest brother Humphrey, Duke of Gloucester, had commissioned a biography of the late king. It was written by one Tito Livio dei Frulovisi, an Italian scholar who was in the duke's service from about 1436. Its purpose was only partly to glorify Henry's memory; it was also intended as an example for his son, the young Henry VI, who by the time it was written was about eighteen and not showing much sign of carrying on where his father left off. Much of the biography is clearly factual, but it follows the classical tradition of inventing speeches for the leading characters to make at the more dramatic moments in the narrative.

Humphrey of Gloucester was a noted patron of the arts, and one of the poets under his wing, the cleric John Lydgate (who had already been commissioned by Henry V to translate a history of the Trojan War), may have been the author of a lengthy poem, 'The Battle of Agincourt', popular in the years after the great victory. A number of surviving Middle English ballads, as well as the more stately 'Agincourt Carol', date from around the same time. A little later, John Page, an ordinary soldier who was an eye-witness to the siege of Rouen in 1418, wrote an account of that event in verse. Page was writing in 1421-22, while Henry was still alive, and his work naturally reflects the most favourable of contemporary attitudes, emphasising the king's virtues both as warrior and as lawgiver:

> He is manful while the war does last,
> And merciful when war is past.

In addition to the balladeers, there were of course contemporary chroniclers, though we should not be misled by the word 'chronicler' into thinking that they were faithful reporters of events. Even those who were present at the Battle of Agincourt, like the anonymous 'Chaplain', saw it only from one viewpoint. Another eye-witness, the Burgundian Jean Le Fèvre de Saint-Remy, was a non-combatant. Saint-Remy tended to take the side of the French, despite Burgundy's alliance with England – as of course, the Chaplain took the side of the English. His fellow-countryman Enguerrand de Monstrelet was less averse to giving some credit to Henry V. It is important to note, however, that these writers were not aiming for impartiality and seldom for historical veracity, though Monstrelet, in particular, makes considerable play of his attention to detail.

Alain Chartier and Robert Blondel were among a number of French writers whose attitude to the English invasion was somewhat ambivalent. Blondel's *Complanctus bonorum Gallicorum* not only chastised the rulers of France for entering into the Treaty of Troyes, which he saw as a sell-out, but also blamed the Armagnac faction – just as many blamed Burgundy – for refusing to mend their differences and thus allowing Henry V to get a foothold in their country. Few of these writers were able to find reasonable fault with the example set by Henry as king.

Before the development of the printing press brought books within the price range of the general populace, works like these were not published in any quantity and thus their dates of origin are always difficult to establish. It is often impossible to identify which works are original and which include content copied from others. It is no accident that so many of the chroniclers were monks, as they were the members of society who were most likely to be literate. John Strecche, for example, was an Augustinian canon at a priory in Kenilworth, where Henry had spent much of his time. This gave him access to information about the king's activities, and perhaps even the occasional personal contact with the king, but it does not guarantee that the stories he heard from the royal household were not false or fanciful.

Peter Basset, one of Henry's early biographers, whose work is believed to have been drawn on by Edward Hall for *Hall's Chronicle*, published in 1548, seems to have been a member of the king's entourage. He was an associate of Sir John Fastolf and probably fought in the Agincourt campaign even if he was not present at the battle. There has been much speculation as to the fate of his original manuscript, but it is no longer available to us. Another of Fastolf's men, William Worcester, produced *Annales rerum Anglicarum* during the reign of Henry VI, and his later writings were apparently intended to spur on King Edward IV to revive England's claim to the French throne. Although not born until the year of Agincourt, he must have been inspired by stories of past glories he had heard from old Sir John. Like so many during the Wars of the Roses, he switched sides depending whether Lancaster or York seemed to have the upper hand at the time, and was prepared to revise his work accordingly.

Nearly a hundred years after his death, Henry V acquired a new admirer in the shape of his namesake, King Henry VIII, whose own father had usurped the throne (or won it fair and square in battle, depending how you looked at it), leaving a new dynasty that sought ways of justifying its own existence. The Tudors had started quietly but would go on to be the most colourful of English dynasties, and Henry VIII was the most memorable of them all. Early in his reign, when he was a headstrong and active youth, Henry V must have looked to him like the perfect example of kingship, and he would have taken the first *Life of Henry V* written in English as a handbook on how to go about it. He was perhaps not mature enough to recognise how much things had changed since the early fifteenth century and understand why the strategy pursued by his very distant cousin was no longer appropriate. The book appears to have been sponsored by the Earl of Ormond, whose ancestor, the fourth earl, had known Henry V in person, but it is mostly hearsay and contains little original material.

Of all the fiction written about King Henry V, it is William Shakespeare's play, *Henry V*, that has coloured our present-day image of Henry most vividly. He was not the only Elizabethan playwright to use the chronicles of English history as source material, and he was not the only one to take Henry V and the Battle of Agincourt as his subject. However, alongside his tour de force, all other adaptations quickly paled into insignificance.

Another prominent Elizabethan dramatist, who enjoyed even greater success in the Jacobean period, was Michael Drayton, who produced both a ballad and a more serious poem on the subject of the Battle of Agincourt. During his career, Drayton wrote a number of works celebrating English medieval history, and it was he who coined the phrase 'Fair stood the wind for France', at the opening of his 1605 ballad. His longer poem, published in 1627, contains graphic descriptions of violence that perhaps come closer to the truth of the battle than the fanciful scenes of individual heroism.

The members of Shakespeare's audience were already familiar with 'Prince Hal' as a character in his *Henry IV* plays. In these, he chose to make the prince a foil for his father, a headstrong young man who consorts with disreputable figures such as Falstaff and his drunken friends at the Boar's Head tavern, run by Mistress Quickly. Despite using this as an opportunity for high comedy, Shakespeare makes it clear in *Henry IV Part I* and *Part II* that the prince has both natural ability and natural nobility, and the final scenes in which, having acceded to the throne, he somewhat callously rejects Falstaff are extremely moving. Some of the fictional characters from Falstaff's retinue reappear in *Henry V* as common soldiers in his army at Agincourt, and one, Bardolph, is hanged for stealing from a church – an incident that we know is based on fact, but which would have had a poignancy for those in the audience who had seen the earlier plays in which Bardolph and Prince Hal were close companions.

In *Henry V*, Shakespeare's attitude to the French is less one-sided than we might expect, and with good reason. Henry V died after reigning for only nine years and enjoying only two years of marriage. He left behind one son, King Henry VI, who was too young to reign in his own right; he was literally a baby. By the time he wrote this, in around 1599, Shakespeare had already completed his cycle of plays about King Henry VI, to which he refers in his epilogue, mentioning what would come next in history, summarising how Henry

> ...left his son imperial lord.
> Henry the Sixth, in infant bands crown'd King
> Of France and England, did this king succeed;
> Whose state so many had the managing,
> That they lost France and made his England bleed:
> Which oft our stage hath shown.

Henry V: A History of His Most Important Places and Events

Although Shakespeare's history plays sometimes do carry a message of encouragement or warning, this is one of the few where the message is so overt. Hence the first major film ever made of the play, at the climax of the Second World War in 1944, is unapologetically patriotic and propagandist. Laurence Olivier, who directed and starred in it, was under orders from the British government to produce something to boost morale, and the film was a massive success on every level, even including a rousing score from classical composer William Walton (already well known for his *Spitfire Prelude*) which remains popular.

Olivier is no exception to the general rule that the star playing Henry V must be handsome. The film was unusual for its time for being made in Technicolor, making the most of the colourful, flattering costumes and 'a cast of thousands', in order to convey the heroism of Henry and his army as fulsomely as possible in a time when the task of arousing patriotic pride in cinema audiences was at its most critical. However, the writers of the screenplay deliberately omitted some scenes that they felt showed the king's less gentlemanly side, such as the executions of Bardolph and the Southampton plotters.

Kenneth Branagh, in making his 1989 film version, had no such political agenda, and the result is a more earthy portrayal that does not shrink from showing violence and bloodshed in a pseudo-realistic manner. It is clearer from this version that the battlefield was a boggy deathtrap, whereas Olivier's battlefield more closely resembles a neatly-trimmed golf course. Nevertheless, it remains a fictional portrait of the king, reproducing Shakespeare's relatively few errors.

In order to conform to the classical unities, for which his use of The Chorus in this play suggests he was aiming, Shakespeare needed to have the action take place within as compact as possible a period of time, and he achieves this by making it appear that Henry's invasion of France follows on almost immediately from his receipt of the Dauphin's tennis balls, and that the Battle of Agincourt is immediately followed by his betrothal to Princess Catherine, rather than revealing that the events of the play actually took place over a period of six years. This one element of the play, more than any other, has contributed to the general belief among the British public that Agincourt was a decisive battle that permanently established England's supremacy over France.

A memorial to Shakespeare at the Bancroft Gardens in Stratford-upon-Avon, designed by Sir Ronald Gower and erected in 1888, shows the bard surrounded by some of the characters he created, including 'Prince Hal', a slim youth raising the crown of England above his head. Although it is an image of the character rather than the historical figure, it is a homage to traditional portraits of the king, notably the pudding-basin haircut.

Almost all film and television adaptations have used Shakespeare's play as the basis of the action, with notable (and good-looking) actors like Robert Hardy (*An Age of Kings*, 1960), David Gwillim (The BBC Television Shakespeare, 1979), Michael Pennington (*The Wars of the Roses*, 1989), and Tom Hiddleston (*The Hollow Crown*, 2012), all taking the lead role. On stage, Ivor Novello (1938) is probably the most unexpected of the great names who have played Henry; others have included Ralph Richardson (1931), Richard Burton (1955), Ian Holm (1965), Timothy Dalton (1972) and Michael Sheen (1997). A later film, *The King* (2019), takes greater liberties with Shakespeare's plays, with Henry (played by a half-French actor) portrayed as an incorrigible layabout who suddenly finds his vocation as a warrior. In this version, the Dauphin becomes a clownish character and Falstaff a more serious one.

After playing the king on stage and screen, Robert Hardy became fascinated by the Battle of Agincourt and the role played in it by the longbow. In 1963 he wrote and presented *The Picardy Affair*, a ground-breaking documentary in which he explored the historical background to the Agincourt campaign, and he learned enough about the longbow to be considered an expert on it, later writing two books on the subject and becoming a consultant to the Mary Rose project in 1982.

Few writers have made a serious attempt to emulate Shakespeare in telling the life story of King Henry V. However, there was a fashion in the seventeenth and eighteenth centuries for writing more accessible versions of Shakespeare's plays. *King Lear* and *Romeo and Juliet* were among the Shakespeare tragedies that were amended to enable a happy ending. Roger Boyle, Earl of Orrery, a politician and part-time playwright, produced his own version of *Henry V* in 1668. The story was substantially changed, and included scenes in which Henry vies for the hand of Catherine of Valois with Owen Tudor – who, to the best of anyone's knowledge, never even saw her until after she became queen consort of England. The reason for this re-telling may have been to highlight the ancestry of the contemporary royal family, that of King Charles II, who was descended not from Henry V but from Catherine and her second husband. Thus a story that might have ended tragically with the death of a king ends with the Battle of Agincourt and with Henry winning his bride, but also with a hint of what is to come.

Quite a number of romantic novelists have chosen to focus, usually rather fancifully, on Henry's relationship with Catherine of Valois. Distinguished historical novelists like Jean Plaidy, Georgette Heyer and Bernard Cornwell have included the king as a character in their books, but rarely is he at the centre of the action. The same is true of John Cowper Powys's novel, *Owen Glendower*, one of few to attempt to depict Henry as a child. A notable exception is Edith Pargeter, who, in addition to her Cadfael series, wrote several historical novels set in her home area, one of which, *A Bloody Field By Shrewsbury* (1972), deals specifically with the early reign of King Henry IV, but has the young Prince Hal as a major character, although secondary to Harry Hotspur.

In the colonial period, a few authors saw Henry V as a good topic for a novel, carrying a suitably moral message (as indeed did many historians of that time). Charlotte M Yonge's 1870 novel, *The Caged Lion*, sees Henry through the eyes of King James I of Scotland, as does Nigel Tranter in his 1967 romantic adventure, *Lion Let Loose*. G A Henty's 1897 children's book, *At Agincourt: A Tale of the White Hoods of Paris*, focuses on the activities of an imaginary man-at-arms who is picked out for special notice by the king and saves his life during the Battle of Agincourt. *Claud the Archer* (1909), a collaboration by three English writers, is another rags-to-riches story, in which a Saxon tenant farmer gets one up on his Norman overlord, although its attitude to war as a concept is less than admiring. At the latter end of the chronological list is the 'graphic novel' by Canadian artist Will Gill, published in 2015 and still concentrating on the one specific battle.

Modern French writers have, naturally, not been keen to make a hero of Henry V, although even contemporary French chroniclers admitted to a grudging admiration of him, both as a king and as a man. Pierre Naudin's 2006 novel, *Le Bourbier d'Azincourt* (*The Quagmire of Agincourt*), is part of a series about the Hundred Years' War, and views both the king and his father with the level of hostility one might expect.

Nevertheless, Henry's heroic reputation has never really gone away. Criticisms of his leadership style, military skill and personality were, and are, vastly outnumbered by works that praise him even where they do not glorify. He remains the most widely-admired of English kings.

Epilogue

Luckily for England, Henry's mother had given birth to several sons, and the younger brothers of King Henry V were able to hold things together while they waited for Henry VI to grow up – but not afterwards, because Henry VI appears to have suffered from some form of mental illness, perhaps inherited from his grandfather, King Charles VI of France, and the end result of his inability to rule effectively was the Wars of the Roses. Yet Shakespeare does not portray Henry as truly mad, just peace-loving, nor does he portray King Charles VI as raving mad.

John, Duke of Bedford, must sometimes have wondered how things would have turned out if his eldest brother had not had a son and he had inherited the throne himself in 1422. Ironically, none of Henry V's three younger brothers, capable as they were, was survived by a legitimate heir, nor indeed were either of their sisters, even though all the siblings had made strategic marriages. Thus the heirs of Henry's traitorous cousin, Richard, Earl of Cambridge, would later be able to exercise their claim to the throne as rivals of the crowned king.

Catherine of Valois, the young widow of King Henry V, despite being the Queen Mother, was regarded with great suspicion because she was French. She had little say in her son's upbringing, and was not allowed to spend much time with him. There were official concerns about her relationship with Edmund Beaufort, Earl of Somerset, a descendant of John of Gaunt on the wrong side of the blanket, and a law was passed effectively preventing her from remarrying legally.

She was given a household at Windsor Castle, and the keeper of that household, the person responsible for looking after Catherine's everyday needs, was a Welshman named Owen Tudor. He was not much older than she was, and is said to have fought at Agincourt, but no one knows for sure. A romance was almost inevitable. It is said that they were secretly married; at least, that is what their children claimed. Over a period of six or seven years, Catherine gave birth to several children, the oldest of whom was Edmund Tudor, the father of King Henry VII and great-grandfather of Queen Elizabeth I. Thus the wheel had come full circle. Henry VII made no extravagant claims to the throne of France on the basis of his descent from King Charles VI, nor did his granddaughter. By that time, the English Crown had lost all its French possessions. So much for the stupendous victory at Agincourt.

To find out more about the Tudor legacy and continue the journey, read Phil Carradice's *Following in the Footsteps of Henry Tudor*, also published by Pen & Sword.

Appendix

How to Follow in the Footsteps of Henry of Monmouth

It has already been stated that it is simply not possible to follow Henry's movements with great exactitude. Most people find it a challenge to visualise the past, and perhaps this is one reason why so many of us have such a fascination with historical figures and events. Whatever we may think we know and however hard we may study, we cannot view the past, and thus we can never be sure what it was really like. At best, we are seeing it through a clouded window. Occasionally the sun comes out and illuminates certain aspects, but only for a moment.

The events and journeys described in this book, although in chronological order, do not need to be followed sequentially, and most readers will not have the time or opportunity to do so. It can be just as interesting to explore the locations Henry knew in adulthood before looking at his childhood haunts, or to investigate the way he died before looking in detail at the battles he won. The places he lived or visited are by no means the whole story, but they are a major part of it.

Anyone who has visited a historic building with good signposting and information panels will have experienced the shock and wonder of new discoveries about how people in past centuries worked, ate, slept, and interacted with one another in their daily life. In France, as in Britain, most towns and cities have undergone enormous changes in terms of the built environment, so that the only enduring landmarks are the church, and sometimes the castle, that were common to every major settlement. These can tell us a lot about the past, but visiting a location that does not contain buildings or visible remains of buildings can be equally rewarding if we allow our imaginations a little freedom.

There are many possible interpretations of the past. The further back we go, the more uncertain we become. The only thing we can be sure of is that we would find living in the fifteenth century quite uncomfortable compared to our modern existence; and yet there may be an 'up' side to it that we find impossible to envisage from this distance in time.

No book can tell Henry's life story comprehensively, and this one does not attempt to do so. Henry was a complex human being, one with many virtues and many failings. If we allowed ourselves to think we have a complete understanding of the man, any more than we have a complete understanding of our closest friend, we would probably be mistaken. The goal of this book is to intrigue more than to educate, to pique the interest rather than to lead the reader down a given path. Most of all, its purpose is to 'entertain' the reader in the true sense of the word: 'entretenir', a French word Henry might have used in conversation, meant 'to maintain'. If this book has maintained your interest, it has achieved its goal without the reader ever having to go outside the front door.

Visitor Locations

Note: Places not listed here may be found in the index.

To follow in Henry's footsteps, driving is generally the most convenient option, since many smaller places will not have a railway station and may not even have a regular bus service. Larger towns and cities, in both the UK and France, will normally be accessible by public transport, but services and timetables are likely to vary in the course of an average year. Cycling is a popular hobby in both countries, and may be an easier option for visits to some of the smaller towns and villages listed.

NOTE: At the time of publication, many visitor centres and sites of interest in the UK and France have been fully or partly closed for a prolonged period in accordance with government regulations. Any opening times and visitor charges listed here are therefore subject to change and should always be checked with the venue before attempting to visit. Where the venue is open, note that advance booking may be required.

Chapter 1: Monmouth area

Public transport: There is no rail passenger service to Monmouth. The nearest railway stations, Lydney (Gloucestershire), Chepstow and Abergavenny, are all within 30 minutes drive.

Both Chepstow and Abergavenny have bus services to Monmouth. National Express buses to Monmouth can be taken from London and Cardiff.

By car: As with most busy towns, parking is not always easy to find, but is not expensive at off-peak times.

Monmouth Festival: The annual Monmouth Festival is mainly a music festival. It is free to attend and therefore attracts many visitors. If you are not interested in the festival, it is best to avoid that period in late July/early August. See the festival website for the latest information: www.monmouthfestival.co.uk

Monmouth Castle and Regimental Museum
Address: Monmouth NP25 3BS

The Regimental Museum of the Royal Monmouthshire Royal Engineers is located in the castle, and is open from 14:00 to 17:00 daily from 1 April to 31 October. It is very small and entry is free.

Monmouth Museum
Address: Priory Street, Monmouth NP25 3XA

The museum, also called The Nelson Museum and Local History Centre, is located in the old Market Hall. It is open daily (except Wednesdays) 11.00 – 16.00. Entry is free.

Shire Hall and Tourist Information Centre
Address: 3 Agincourt Square, Monmouth NP25 3DY

The Shire Hall, built in 1724, has a statue of Henry V on its façade, but otherwise has no connection with the king. It does contain a commemorative tapestry and small exhibitions about Henry V and Geoffrey of Monmouth, as well as the town's Tourist Information Office. Normal opening times are 10.00 am - 4.00 pm.

Courtfield (Welsh Bicknor)
For visitors without private transport, visiting Welsh Bicknor is difficult and time-consuming. Buses do run to the village from Monmouth and Gloucester, but the journey time is excessive for the distance involved. Keen walkers may make the eight-mile journey on foot, but are unlikely to find any overnight accommodation in the village itself.

Chapter 2: Prince of Wales

Chester Castle
Website: https://www.english-heritage.org.uk/visit/places/chester-castle-agricola-tower-and-castle-walls

Address: Grosvenor St, Chester CH1 2DN

Entrance fee payable

Leicester Castle
Website: https://leicestercastle.co.uk/
Address: 7 Castle View, Leicester LE1 5WH

De Montfort University Heritage Centre
Opening hours: Tuesday to Friday, 12.00 pm to 5.00 pm.

E-mail: heritage@dmu.ac.uk

Address: Hawthorn Building, De Montfort University, The Newarke, Leicester LE2 7DR

The Queen's College, Oxford
Address: High St, Oxford OX1 4AW

Visits by members of the public can be arranged through the Tourist Information Office, 15-16 Broad Street, Oxford OX1 4AS (info@experienceoxfordshire.org).

Chapter 3: Shrewsbury and area

Public transport: Rail services to Shrewsbury run from Aberystwyth, Birmingham, Cardiff, Chester, Hereford, Manchester, Wolverhampton and Wrexham.

There are many, and frequent, local bus services to Shrewsbury. National Express buses to Shrewsbury can be taken directly from Aberystwyth, and from other destinations via Wolverhampton.

By car: For those not wishing to stay overnight, the Harlescott park & ride bus service is based at the supermarket (Battlefield SY1 4HA), which allows visitors to combine a visit to Shrewsbury with a visit to the site of the battle.

Battlefield 1403 Visitor Centre and Church of St Mary Magdalene
Address: Battlefield, Shropshire, SY4 3DB

In addition to an exhibition, the visitor centre has a farm shop, butchery, deli and café. Opening hours for the visitor centre are Monday to Saturday 9.30 am - 7.30 pm and Sunday 10.00 am - 14.00 pm.

Outside the church is a statue of King Henry IV. The roof beams are decorated with the shields of knights who fought with Henry IV at the Battle of Shrewsbury. A service is held each July to commemorate the anniversary of the battle. The key to the church is kept at the Battlefield 1403 Visitor Centre, about 100 yards away.

The church and visitor centre are three miles from Shrewsbury railway station. Bus routes no 511 (via Wem to Whitchurch), and 64 (via Shawbury to Market Drayton) take passengers to a spot approximately one mile from the church.

Haughmond Abbey (English Heritage)
Address: Upton Magna, Uffington, Shropshire, SY4 4RW
Open 10.00 - 16.00 daily. Entry is free.

Town Walls Tower (National Trust)
Address: Town Walls, Shrewsbury SY1 1TN
Open about eight times a year.

St Alkmund's Church
Address: St Alkmunds Square, Shrewsbury SY1 1UH
Open daily. Entry is free.

St Giles Church
Address: 29 Wenlock Rd, Shrewsbury SY2 6JP

St Julian's Church
Address: St Alkmunds Square, Shrewsbury SY1 1UH
Privately owned. Not currently open to the public.

St Mary the Virgin
Address: St Mary's Street, Shrewsbury, Shropshire, SY1 1DX
Free entry
Note: No longer in use as a church, but contains a cafe and shop.

St Winifred's Well, Woolston, Shropshire
Address: Woolston Bank Cottages, Woolston, Oswestry SY10 8HZ

Private, available to rent from Landmark Trust.

St Winifred's Well, Holywell, Flintshire
Address: Plessington House, Greenfield St, Holywell CH8 7PN

Open: 09:00 - 16:30 daily.

Chapter 4: Campaigning in Wales

Aberystwyth Castle
Address: Aberystwyth, Ceredigion SY23 2AG

Open site; free entry.

Coity Castle
Address: Coity, Bridgend CF35 6BG

Open site; free entry.

Beverley Minster
Address: Highgate, Beverley, East Yorkshire HU17 0DP

E-mail: minster@beverleyminster.org.uk

Open to the public most days.

Harlech Castle (CADW)
Address: Harlech Castle, Harlech LL46 2YH

Opening times vary depending on time of year. Entrance fee payable.

Chapter 5: Early Kingship

Kenilworth Castle
Address: Castle Road, Kenilworth, Warwickshire, CV8 1NE
Open

London

British Library
Website: https://www.bl.uk/

Address: 96 Euston Road, London NW1 2DB

The British Library contains medieval manuscripts that can throw light on the period in which Henry of Monmouth lives. Many of these can be viewed online.

Note: The library is open to the public free of charge, but arrangements must be made beforehand by those wishing to view any of the 170 million items in the library's collection.

Eltham Palace (English Heritage)
Address: Court Yard, London SE9 5QE

Opening times vary depending on time of year. Entrance fee payable.

Lambeth Palace
Address: Lambeth Palace, London SE1 7JU

Private: open to the public only for pre-arranged guided tours, open days and special events.

St Paul's Cathedral
Address: St. Paul's Churchyard, London EC4M 8AD

Open every day 10 am - 4.30 pm. Entrance fee payable except for those attending services.

Syon Abbey/Syon House
The abbey founded by Henry V in 1415 was moved to a nearby location in 1431 and no longer stands. The Georgian mansion, owned by the Duke of Northumberland, was built on the site of the second abbey after it was destroyed during the Reformation.

Address: Syon House, Syon Park, Brentford, Middlesex TW8 8JF

Website: https://www.syonpark.co.uk/

Opening times vary. Entrance fee payable.

Westminster Abbey
Address: 20 Deans Yard, Westminster, London SW1P 3PA

Opening times vary.

Entrance fee payable (plus additional fee for the Queen's Diamond Jubilee Galleries).

Website: https://www.westminster-abbey.org

E-mail: info@westminster-abbey.org

Chapter 6: Agincourt campaign

"Agincourt Wales Trail": https://www.visitmonmouthshire.com/things-to-do/agincourt.aspx

Public transport
If not travelling by car, the quickest way to reach Harfleur is to take a flight to Deauville or Paris. Buses run from Deauville to Le Havre. Trains run from Paris and Deauville to both Le Havre and Harfleur. Reaching the site of the Battle of Agincourt by public transport is difficult.

Coach tour
Another option for those without their own transport is to join one of the many tours of Normandy that are available. Although most of these tend to concentrate on the battlefields and cemeteries of two World Wars, there is a variety of itineraries, many of them passing through or near towns and cities where Henry V campaigned. Some tour operators will even go out of their way to help passengers see individual sites in which they are particularly interested.

Private car

If travelling by car, the options for crossing the channel are Eurostar or ferry. Ferries run from Newhaven to Dieppe and from Portsmouth to Le Havre, these being the two most convenient ports for exploring the area around Harfleur. For those who prefer to concentrate on Agincourt, Calais will be more convenient.

Note: The places on Henry's route are listed below in alphabetical, rather than chronological, order:

Acheux-en-Amiénois

Château de l'Épine

Address: 3 Rue Raymond de Wazières, 80560 Acheux-en-Amiénois, France

Athies

Remains of town walls can be seen in Rue Chemin sous la ville and Rue de Ste Radegonde, near the church of Notre Dame de l'Assomption.

Address: Rue Chemin sous la ville, 80200 Athies, France

Azincourt and Maisoncelle

The modern Agincourt monument is at Maisoncelle. It dates from 1963.

Address: 62310 Maisoncelle, France

An older memorial in the form of a 'calvary' or public crucifix, dating from the 1860s, can be seen by the roadside on the D104, on the site of a former memorial chapel.

Address: Hameau de la Gacogne, 62310 Azincourt, France

Caix

Church of Ste Croix

Address: Rue des Fleurons, 80170 Caix, France

Calais
Église Notre-Dame de Calais

Address: 17 Rue Notre Dame, 62100 Calais, France

Tour du Guet (Watchtower)

Address: Place d'Armes, 62100 Calais, France

Corbie
Abbey Saint-Pierre

Address: 12 Rue Charles de Gaulle, 80800 Corbie, France

Partial remains of town wall

Address: Rue de l'Enclos, 80800 Corbie, France

Eaucourt-sur-Somme
Chateau Eaucourt-sur-Somme

Address: Rue du Pont, 80580 Eaucourt-sur-Somme, France

The chateau is a ruin, but tours can be arranged in the summer months.

Eu
Church of Notre-Dame et Saint Laurent.

Address: 4 Place Guillaume le Conquerant, 76260 Eu, France

Frévent
Abbaye Notre-Dame de Cercamp

Address: Rue du Général de Gaulle, 62270 Frévent, Pas-de-Calais, France

Guînes DU CHÂTEAU 62340 GUÎNES
Tour de l'Horloge de Guînes

Address: Rue du Château, 62340 GUÎNES, France

Website: http://www.tour-horloge-guines.com/

Harfleur

Museum of the Priory (archaeology of Harfleur)

Address: 50 rue de la République, 76700 Harfleur

Phone : 06 16 33 43 01 - 02 35 45 40 62

Email : musee@harfleur.fr

Website : http://www.harfleur.fr

Graville Abbey
Address: Rue de l'Abbaye 76600 Le Havre

Phone: 02 35 42 27 90

Open 10.00-12.30 pm and 13.45-18.00, 1 April to 3 November inclusive except Tuesdays and public holidays

Parc de la Ferme du Mont Lecomte

Address:

Rue Fourier, 76610 LE HAVRE

209 Rue Edouard Vaillant, 76610 LE HAVRE (alternative)

Nesle (not to be confused with Nesles, near Calais)
Château Boisset (fragmentary ruins).

Address: Place de la République, 80190 Nesle, France

Péronne
Historial de la Grande Guerre (in the castle)

Address: Place André Audinot, 80200 Péronne, France

Chapter 7-8: Later French campaigns

Argentan
Tour Marguerite (Marguerite Tower)

Address: Rue de la Vicomté, 61200 Argentan, France

Château des Ducs (Palais de Justice)

Address: Boulevard du Général de Gaulle, 61200 Argentan, France

Bernay

Abbaye Notre-Dame de Bernay

Address: Place Gustave Heon, 27300 Bernay, France

Open to visitors daily in summer; gardens open throughout the year. Entrance fee payable.

Museum of Beaux-Arts

Address: Place Guillaume de Volpiano, 27300 Bernay, France

Bonneville-sur-Touques

Château de Bonneville-sur-Touques (Château de Guillaume-le-Conquérant)

Address: 27270 Chamblac, France

Caen

Château de Caen, 14000 Caen, France

Entrance to the ramparts is free.

The Musée des Beaux-Arts de Caen (rebuilt 1971) and the Musée de Normandie are within the castle precincts.

Abbaye aux Hommes

Address: Esplanade Jean-Marie Louvel, 14027 Caen, France

Open to visitors daily in summer.

Entrance fee payable.

Abbaye aux Dames

Address: Place Reine Mathilde, 14000 Caen, France

Church of St Étienne le Vieux (not to be confused with the abbey)

Church of St Jean

Address: 110 Rue Saint-Jean, 14000 Caen, France

Chartres
Centre International du Vitrail

Address: 5 Rue du Cardinal Pie, 28000 Chartres, France

Cathedral of Notre-Dame de Chartres

Address:

Old city walls
Address: Rue de la Porte Guillaume, 28000 Chartres, France

Évreux

Notre-Dame d'Évreux

Address: Rue Charles Corbeau, 27000 Évreux, France

Bishop's Palace Museum

Address: 2 Esplanade Anne Baudot, 27000 Évreux, France

Falaise
Château Guillaume-le-Conquérant, Place Guillaume le Conquérant, 14700 Falaise, France

Open: 10.00 - 18.00 daily (19:00 in July/August). Entry charge.

Website: www.chateau-guillaume-leconquerant.fr/

Louviers
Notre-Dame de Louviers

Address: Place du Parvis Notre Dame, 27400 Louviers, France

Mantes
Collegiale Notre-Dame de Mantes

Address: Place de l'Etape, 78200 Mantes-la-Jolie

Melun
Collégiale Notre-Dame de Melun

Address:

1 rue de la Courtille, 77000 Melun, France

Musée de Melun

Address: Maison de la Vicomté, 4 quai de la Courtille, 77000 Melun, France

Prieuré Saint-Sauveur

Address: Rue du Château, 77000 Melun, France

Rouen
Abbey of Saint-Ouen

Address: Place du Général de Gaulle, 76000 Rouen, France

Limited opening hours; free entry.

L'église Sainte-Jeanne-d'Arc (Church of Joan of Arc)

Address: Place du Vieux Marché, 76000 Rouen, France

Free entry.

Gros-Horloge

Address: Rue du Gros-Horloge, 76000 Rouen, France

Opening hours vary; entrance fee payable.

Historial Jeanne d'Arc

Website: http://www.historial-jeannedarc.fr/

Address: 7, Rue Saint-Romain, 76000 Rouen, France

Open Tuesday to Sunday; entrance fee payable.

Notre-Dame de Rouen

Address: Place de la Cathédrale, 76000 Rouen, France

Limited opening hours; free entry.

Tour Jeanne d'Arc (former keep of Rouen Castle)

Address: Rue Bouvreuil, 76000 Rouen, France

Limited opening hours; entrance fee payable.

Troyes

Cathédrale Saint-Pierre-et-Saint-Paul de Troyes

Address: Place Saint-Pierre, 10000 Troyes, France

Limited opening hours; free entry.

Church of Saint-Jean-du-Marché de Troyes

Address: 78 Rue Urbain IV, 10000 Troyes, France

Gisors

Château Fort de Gisors

Address: Place de Blanmont, 27140 Gisors France

Chapel Saint-Luc (lepers' chapel)

Address: 18-22 Rue de Rouen, 27140 Gisors, France

Occasionally open to the public.

Collegiate Church Saint-Gervais-Saint-Protais

Address: Rue Saint Gervais, 27140 Gisors France

Meaux
Bossuet Garden

Address:

5 place Charles de Gaulle, 77100 Meaux

Opening hours: 8.00 am - 7.00 pm between 1 April and 31 October.

Montereau
Église Notre-Dame et Saint-Loup de Montereau

Address: 1 Rue Jean Jaurès, 77130 Montereau-Fault-Yonne, France

Nemours
Château de Nemours

Address: Rue gautier 1er, 77140 Nemours, France

Paris
Basilica of Saint-Denis

Address: 1 Rue de la Légion d'Honneur, 93200 Saint-Denis, France

Chapelle Saint-Aignan

Address: 26 Rue Chanoinesse, 75004 Paris, France

Opening: The chapel is open only once a year, on the feast of Saint Aignan of Orleans (17 November).

Conciergerie and Sainte-Chapelle

Address: 2 Boulevard du Palais, 75001 Paris, France

Louvre
Address: Rue de Rivoli, 75001 Paris, France

Maison d'Héloïse et d'Abélard

Address: 11 Quai aux Fleurs, 75004 Paris, France

Notre-Dame de Paris

Address: 6 Parvis Notre-Dame - Pl. Jean-Paul II, 75004 Paris, France

Old city walls (Wall of Philip Augustus)

Address: 75004 Paris, France

Tour Jean-sans-Peur

Address: 20 Rue Étienne Marcel, 75002 Paris, France

Pontoise
Chateau de Pontoise

Address: 96 Rue de Vauréal, 95000 Cergy, France

Senlis
Abbey church of St Vincent

Address: 30 Rue de Meaux, 60300 Senlis

Castle and remains of city walls

Address: Place du Parvis de la cathédrale Notre Dame, 60300 Senlis, France

Cathedral
Address: Place Notre-Dame, 60300 Senlis, France

Sens
Cathedral of Saint-Étienne de Sens

Address: Place de la République, 89100 Sens, France

Museum of Sens

Address: 135 Rue Déportés et de la Résistance, 89100 Sens, France

Tour de la Breche and remains of city walls

Address: Boulevard du 14 juillet, 89100 Sens, France

Vernon-sur-Seine
Chateau des Tourelles

Address: 4 Rue Ogereau, 27200 Vernon, France

Maison du Temps Jadis

Address: Rue Saint-Sauveur, 27200 Vernon, France

Tour des Archives
Address: 14 Rue des Écuries des Gardes, 27200 Vernon, France

Vincennes
Chateau de Vincennes

Address: Avenue de Paris, 94300 Vincennes, France

Entrance fee.

Other Places of Interest

English Heritage sites
Portchester Castle
Address: Church Road, Portchester, Hampshire, PO16 9QW

Titchfield Abbey
Address: Mill Lane, Titchfield, Hampshire, PO15 5RA

Wolvesey Castle
Address: College Street, Winchester, Hampshire, SO23 9NB:

Private properties open to the public
Canterbury Cathedral
Address: The Precincts, Canterbury CT1 2EH

Tel: +44 (0) 1227 865279 (Welcome Centre)

Entry fee payable.

In addition to the tomb of Thomas Becket, Canterbury Cathedral contains two important tombs: those of Henry V's father, King Henry IV (the only monarch buried there) and Henry's great-uncle, Edward, the Black Prince.

Battle of Agincourt

For those interested in the men who participated in the battle, the 'Agincourt Roll' (Harley 782, a manuscript produced over a hundred years after the battle) survives in the British Library, and an online database, representing a cumulative record of the names on contemporary muster rolls, has been created by the National Archives at Kew.

All Souls' College, Oxford, OX1 4AL, was founded by King Henry VI in 1438, a mere thwenty-three years after the Battle of Agincourt, when many of the participants were still in the prime of life. It contained a chantry chapel which was to be a permanent memorial to those killed in the Hundred Years' War. It is open to the general public (maximum group size is six) 14.00 - 16.00 on weekdays and Sunday at times when the College is open. This excludes many public holidays and the whole of August, so it is advisable to check in advance before attempting to visit.

Below is a list of some of the more prominent participants on the English side, along with details of where their tombs or memorials can be found. In many cases, only the bones of those killed were returned home for burial. In some cases, the tomb is empty or has been destroyed. For addresses and postcodes of larger churches, see the chapter lists above.

Memorials to Henry V:
- Strawberry Hill House, Twickenham, London TW1 4ST – Victorian stained glass window with image of Henry V. Open to the public (entry fee payable).
- York Minster, Deangate, York, YO1 7HH – sculpture of Henry V among other English kings on the choir screen (entry fee payable).

Died during the campaign:
- William Boteler – not known; family tombs are to be seen at St Elphin's Church, Warrington, Cheshire WA1 2TL
- Sir Edward Burnell, son-in-law of the 2nd Earl of Suffolk – no known tomb
- Sir Nicholas Haute – no known tomb
- Sir Thomas Clinton, MP – St Mary's Church, Hunton, Maidstone, Kent, ME15 0RR (memorial)
- Richard Courtenay, Bishop of Norwich – Westminster Abbey
- Thomas Fitzalan, 5th Earl of Arundel – Arundel Chapel, St Nicholas's Church, London Road, Arundel, West Sussex BN18 9AT
- Sir Nicholas de Longford – St Chad's Church, Long Lane Longford, Ashbourne, Derbyshire DE6 3DS (effigy)
- Sir John Phelip – St Mary & All Saints, Kidderminster, Worcestershire DY10 2JN
- Michael de la Pole, 2nd Earl of Suffolk – St Andrew's Church, Wingfield, Suffolk IP21 5RA
- Sir Robert de Tye – Holy Trinity Church, Barsham, Suffolk NR34 8HA

Killed in the battle:
- Edward, Duke of York – Church of St Mary & All Saints, Fotheringhay, Northamptonshire PE8 5HZ (memorial)
- Dafydd Gam – commemorated by stained glass window in St Teilo's Church, Llantilio Crossenny NP7 8SY
- Sir Richard de Keighley of Inskip – no known tomb
- Michael de la Pole, 3rd Earl of Suffolk – St Mary the Virgin, Ewelme, Oxfordshire OX10 6HS
- Roger Vaughan of Bredwardine – effigy in St Andrew's Church, Bredwardine, Herefordshire HR3 6BT

Survived the battle/campaign:
- Sir Robert Babthorpe (died 1436) – St Mary the Virgin, Hemingbrough, North Yorkshire YO8 6QU (no visible memorial)

- Thomas Beaufort, Earl of Dorset (later Duke of Exeter; died 1426) – Bury St Edmunds Abbey, Angel Hill, Bury St Edmunds Suffolk IP33 1LS. Beaufort's embalmed body was accidentally discovered in 1772, and was reburied 'near the north-east pillar' (no visible memorial)
- John Duke of Bedford (died 1435) – Rouen Cathedral, France
- Sir Ralph Boteler (later Baron Sudeley; died 1473) – not known
- Humphrey, Duke of Gloucester (died 1447) – St Albans Cathedral, Hertfordshire AL1 1BY
- Thomas Camoys, 1st Baron Camoys (died 1421) - St George's Church, Petersfield Road, Trotton, West Sussex GU31 5EN
- John Clifford, 7th Baron Clifford (died 1422) – Bolton Priory, North Yorkshire (St. Mary and St. Cuthbert Priory Churchyard) BD23 6AL
- Sir Robert Corbet (died 1420) – St Bartholomew Church, Moreton Corbet, Shropshire SY4 4DW (no tomb, but Corbet Chapel survives)
- Sir John Cornwall of Ampthill Castle (later Baron Fanhope; died 1443) – cemetery of the Black Friars, Ludgate, London (tomb does not survive)
- Richard de Vere, 11th Earl of Oxford (died 1417) – Colne Priory, later moved to St Stephen's Chapel, Bures St Mary, Suffolk CO8 5LD
- Sir Thomas Erpingham (died 1428) – Norwich Cathedral (the Erpingham Gate was also built by him)
- Sir John Fastolf (died 1459) – St Benet's Abbey (ruined, tomb does not survive)
- Sir Simon Felbrigg(e) (died 1442) – memorial (with his first wife) at St Margaret's Church, Felbrigg, Norfolk NR11 8PR. Sir Simon was not buried there, but at the Blackfriars in Norwich, and his tomb does not survive.
- James Fiennes of Herstmonceux (later Baron Saye and Sele; died 1450) – Greyfriars, London (tomb does not survive)

- John Grey, Earl of Tankerville (died 1421) – not known
- Sir William Har(r)ington (died 1440), the king's standard-bearer – St Wilfrid's Churchyard, Main Street, Melling, Lancashire LA6 2RA (no visible tomb)
- Sir Walter Hungerford (later Baron Hungerford; died 1449) – Salisbury Cathedral
- John Holland, Earl of Huntingdon (later Duke of Exeter; died 1447) – Chapel of St. Peter ad Vincula, Tower of London (effigy)
- Sir Piers Legh of Lyme Hall (died 1422) – Legh Chapel, St Michael's Church, Market Place, Macclesfield SK10 1DY (plaque only)
- Sir Rowland Lenthall of Hampton Court Castle (died 1450) – not known
- Thomas Montagu, 4th Earl of Salisbury (died 1428) – Bisham Priory, Berkshire (tomb lost along with church)
- Thomas Morley, 4th Baron Morley (died 1416) – Church of St Mary the Virgin and St Augustine (Austin Friars church), Norwich. The church was demolished in 1547, but a memorial marks the position of the cemetery.
- Edmund Mortimer, 5th Earl of March (died 1426) – Clare Priory, St Edmundsbury Borough, Suffolk CO10 8NX (tomb does not survive; plaque only)
- Sir Lewis Robessart (died 1430), later Baron Bourchier – Westminster Abbey
- Sir John Savage (died 1450), half-brother of Sir Piers Legh – St Michael's Church, Macclesfield
- Thomas of Lancaster (died 1421), brother of Henry V – Canterbury Cathedral
- Sir William ap Thomas (died 1445) – Abergavenny Priory, 5 Monk St, Abergavenny NP7 5ND
- William Troutbeck, Chamberlain of Chester (died 1437 or 1439) – St Mary-on-the-Hill (former Church), Chester CH1 2DW

- Sir Robert de Urswyk, Sheriff of Lancashire (died 1420) – not known

Burial places of other significant figures not involved in the Agincourt campaign
- Edward the Black Prince (died 1376), great-uncle of Henry V – Canterbury Cathedral (Trinity Chapel)
- John of Gaunt (died 1399), grandfather of Henry V – St Paul's Cathedral (tomb destroyed in the Great Fire of London; plaque marks its location)
- King Henry IV of England (died 1413), father of Henry V – Canterbury Cathedral (Trinity Chapel)
- Mary de Bohun (died 1394), mother of Henry V – Church of the Annunciation of Our Lady of the Newarke, Leicester
- John, Duke of Bedford (died 1435), brother of Henry V – Rouen Cathedral (tomb destroyed but a plaque marks its location)
- Blanche of Lancaster (died 1409), sister of Henry V – Church of St Egidius, Neustadt an der Weinstrasse, Germany
- Philippa of Lancaster (died 1430), sister of Henry V – Cloister Church, Vadstena, Sweden
- King Henry VI of England (1421-1471), son of Henry V – St George's Chapel, Windsor
- Humphrey, Earl of Buckingham (died 1399), cousin of King Henry V – Walden Abbey, Saffron Walden, Essex (church and tomb destroyed)
- King Charles VI of France (died 1422) and Queen Isabeau (died 1435), parents-in-law of King Henry V – Basilica of Saint-Denis, Paris
- King Charles VII of France (1403-1461), formerly the Dauphin Charles, brother-in-law of King Henry V – Basilica of Saint-Denis, Paris
- Louis of Guyenne (died 1415), brother-in-law of King Henry V – Notre-Dame de Paris (destroyed)

- John, Duke of Touraine (died 1417), brother-in-law of King Henry V – Abbey of Saint-Corneille (tomb destroyed)
- John the Fearless, Duke of Burgundy (died 1467) – Musée des Beaux-Arts de Dijon (reconstructed tomb moved from its original site)
- Philip the Good, Duke of Burgundy (died 1467) – tomb lost; no funerary monument ever built
- King James I of Scotland (1394-1437) – Perth Charterhouse (destroyed c.1600). A search for the site of James's tomb was launched in 2017.
- The Southampton Plotters: Richard, Duke of Cambridge; Thomas Gray; Henry Scrope, Lord Scrope of Masham (all died 1415) – Leper's Squint Stoup Monument at St Julien's Church, Winkle St, Southampton SO14 2NY (19th century)
- William Alnwick, Archdeacon of Salisbury, later a bishop (died 1449) – Lincoln Cathedral, Lincoln LN2 1PX (tomb destroyed)
- Thomas Arundel, Archbishop of Canterbury (died 1414) – Canterbury Cathedral (under the nave; no effigy)
- Richard Beauchamp, 13th Earl of Warwick (died 1439) – St Mary's Church, Old Square, Warwick CV34 4RA
- Henry Beaufort, Bishop of Winchester (died 1447) – Winchester Cathedral, 9 The Close, Winchester SO23 9LS (entrance fee)
- Henry Chichele, Archbishop of Canterbury (died 1443) – Canterbury Cathedral (North Quire Aisle)
- Constance of York, Countess of Gloucester (died 1416) – Reading Abbey (ruined; tomb does not survive) RG1 3HW
- Elizabeth Mortimer (died 1417) – St George's Church, Trotton, West Sussex
- Sir John Oldcastle (died 1417) – St Giles-in-the-Fields, Camden, London WC2H 8LG (churchyard – not marked)
- Henry Percy, 1st Earl of Northumberland (died 1408) – Alnwick Abbey, Northumberland (only gatehouse still standing)

How to Follow in the Footsteps of Henry of Monmouth

- Henry Percy ('Harry Hotspur') (died 1403) – York Minster (entrance fee)
- Henry Percy, 2nd Earl of Northumberland (died 1455) – St Alban's Abbey
- John Talbot, Earl of Shrewsbury (died 1453) – St Alkmund's Church, Church Street Whitchurch, Shropshire SY13 1LB

Select Bibliography

Primary sources

Gesta Henrici Quinti (The deeds of Henry the Fifth) / translated from the Latin, with introd. and notes by Frank Taylor and John S. Roskell.
Tito Livio Frulovisi, *Vita et Gesta Henrici Quinti*
Enguerrand Monstrelet, *Chronique*
William Noel Sainsbury (ed.) *Calendar of state papers, Volume 2.* Public Record Office, 1873.
Thomas Walsingham, *Historia Anglicana*
Jean de Wavrin, *Recueil des croniques et anchiennes istories de la Grant Bretaigne*

Secondary sources

Battle of Agincourt
Alfred H Burne, *The Agincourt War.* Greenwood Press, 1956
Stephen Cooper, *Agincourt: Myth and Reality 1415-2015.* Pen & Sword, 2014
Anne Curry, *The Battle of Agincourt: Sources and Interpretations*
Peter Hoskins & Anne Curry, *Agincourt 1415: a tourist's guide to the campaign.* Pen & Sword, 2014. ISBN 978 1 78383 157 9
Ian Mortimer, *1415: Henry V's Year of Glory*

General

Books
Christopher Allmand, *Henry V.* Yale University Press, 1993. ISBN 978-0520082939

Select Bibliography

Juliet Barker, *Conquest: the English kingdom of France in the Hundred Years War.* Abacus, 2010. ISBN 978-0349122021

Helen Castor, *Blood and roses.* Faber & Faber, 2005. ISBN 978-0571216710

R R Davies, *Owain Glyndŵr: Prince of Wales*

Keith Dockray, *Henry V.* Tempus, 2004. ISBN 0 7524 3046 7

Gwilym Dodd & Douglas Biggs (ed.), *Henry IV: The Establishment of the Regime, 1399-1406*

Gwilym Dodd (ed.), *Henry V: New Interpretations*

Anthony Emery, *Greater Medieval Houses of England and Wales, 1300–1500: Volume 3, Southern ...*

Anthony Emery, *Seats of Power in Europe during the Hundred Years War.* Oxbow Books, 2016. ISBN 978 1 78570 103 0

Deborah Fisher, *Princes of Wales.* University of Wales Press, 2006. ISBN 978-0708320037

Deborah Fisher, *Royal Wales.* University of Wales Press, 2010. ISBN 978-0708322147

Eddie Jones, *England's Last Medieval Monastery: Syon Abbey 1415–2015*

Lisa Hilton, *Queens Consort.* Weidenfeld & Nicolson, 2008. ISBN 9780753826119

Adrian Pettifer, *Welsh Castles: A Guide by Counties.* Boydell Press, 2000. ISBN 978-0851157788

Kathleen Spaltro & Noeline Bridge, *Royals of England: A Guide for Readers, Travelers, and Genealogists* iUniverse, 2005. ISBN 978-0595373123

Jonathan Sumption, *The Hundred Years War, Volume 4: Cursed Kings* Faber & Faber, 2016. ISBN 978-0571274567

James Endell Tyler, *Henry of Monmouth: Or, Memoirs of the Life and Character of Henry the Fifth, as Prince of Wales and King of England* (1838)

Malcolm Vale, *Henry V: The Conscience of a King.* Yale University Press, 2016. ISBN 978-0300148732

Articles

Ralph A Griffiths, 'Owain Glyndwr and the siege of Coity Castle.' *Morgannwg*, vol 45, page 4.

Anne Curry and Adrian Bell (ed.), 'Soldiers, Weapons and Armies in the Fifteenth Century', *Journal of Medieval Military History,* vol. IX

John Jenkins, 'Modelling the Cult of Thomas Becket in Canterbury Cathedral', *Journal of the British Archaeological Association*, vol. 173:1, pages 100-123

Other media

Eric Zingraff, *Paris au Moyen-Age* and *Paris au Fil de l'eau* (DVD). Grez productions, 2013

Index

Abbeville, 71
Aberystwyth, 34-6, 65, 166, 168
   Castle, 34-5
Acton, Sir Roger, 46
Adam of Usk, 21, 25, 39, 94
Agincourt (Azincourt), 78, 80, 83, 86, 171
   Battle of, vii-viii, 3, 6, 18, 33, 35, 38, 50, 54-8, 66-8, 70, 77-80, 83-6, 89-90, 93, 95-7, 100-1, 106, 112, 115-6, 119, 129, 134, 138, 144, 149, 152-61, 170-1, 181-5
Albert, 75
Alençon, 101
Alnwick, William, 47, 186
Anjou (duchy), 61
Anne of Bohemia, queen consort of England, 48
Anne of Burgundy, 117
Ante (river), 102
Antoine, Duke of Brabant, 84
Aquitaine, 39-40, 64
Argentan, 100-1, 173-4
Arthur of Richemont, 85, 118
Arundel, Thomas, 37, 42, 186
Attingham Park, 20
Avranches, 103

Babthorp(e), Sir Robert, 106, 182
Badby, John, 45
Basset, Peter, 153

Bayeux, 100, 103
   Cathedral, 100
   Tapestry, 100
Beauchamp, Richard, Earl of Warwick, 24, 33-4, 37, 46, 56, 88, 103, 105-6, 114-7, 186
Beauchamp, Richard, Earl of Worcester, 144-5
Beaufort, Edmund, Earl of Somerset, 160
Beaufort, Henry, 11, 37, 40, 47, 61, 139, 186
Beaufort, Thomas, Earl of Dorset, later Duke of Exeter, 68-9, 90, 103, 106, 111, 143, 149, 183
Becket, Thomas, 89, 121, 181
Berkerolles, Sir Laurence, 31-2
Béthune (river), 71
Beverley
   Minster, 137-8, 168
   St John of, 35, 91, 137-8
Biscay, Bay of, 64
Blackheath, 90, 135
Blanche of Lancaster, 1, 3, 7, 51
Blanche of England, Princess (sister of Henry V), 8, 144, 185
Blanchetaque, 71
Blondel, Robert, 152-3
Blount, Sir Walter, 25
Bohun, Mary de (mother of Henry V), 1, 3, 7-8, 10, 15, 185
Boisratier, Guillaume de, 61

Bordeaux, 64
Boucicaut, Marshal, 67, 74, 83, 85
Boulogne, 64
Bouteiller, Guy de, 107
Boyle, Roger, Earl of Orrery, 158
Bradmore, John, 27-9, 51
Branagh, Kenneth, 54, 156
Brecon, 56
Bresle (river), 71
Bridget, St (Bridgettine order), 46-8
Bridlington Priory, 137
Bromley, John, 72
Builth Castle, 45
Byfleet, 49

Caen, 97-99, 102-103, 111, 174-175
Calais, ix, 38, 46, 49, 66, 69-72, 74, 76, 84, 86-9, 93-4, 135, 140, 149, 171-2
Caldicot, 57
Camoys, Lord, 81, 183
Canterbury, 89, 91-4
 Cathedral, 42, 180-181, 185-6
Carmarthen, 56
Castle, Roger, 52
Catherine of Pomerania, 16-17
Catherine of Valois, queen consort of England, ix, 57, 60-1, 114-5, 119-23, 132-9, 145-50, 156, 158, 160-1
Catton, William, 63
Charles d'Orléans, 16, 59, 85
Charles II of England, King, 158
Charles V of France, King, 50, 128, 130, 133-4, 147-8
Charles VI of France, King, 16, 58, 61, 77, 108, 127, 129-132, 146-148, 160-1, 185

Charles VII of France, King ("the Dauphin Charles"), 106, 108, 112, 121, 123, 130, 140, 142, 146-8, 185
Chartier, Alain, 100, 152
Chartres, 140-1, 175
Château Gaillard, 111, 114
Chaucer, Geoffrey, 9, 127
Cheapside, 90
Cheshire, 23, 40, 72
Chester, 18, 26, 29, 33, 165
Cheylesmore, 40
Chichele, Henry, 89, 93, 136, 186
Cirencester, 44
Clifford, Richard, 47
Coity Castle, 31, 168
Constance, Countess of Gloucester, 30, 186
Constance of Castile, 51
Conway Castle, 13
Corbet, Sir Robert, 14, 183
Corbie, 72, 81, 172
Cornwall, John, 144
Courtenay, Richard (Bishop), 37, 142, 189
Courtfield, 2, 8-10, 14, 38, 165
Crécy, Battle of, 56

d'Albret, Charles, Constable of France, 83-4
Dafydd Gam, 33, 56, 182
David of Scotland, King, 26
Dieppe, 71, 111, 171
Dover, 38, 89, 93-4, 135, 140, 149
Drayton, Michael, 154
Dubricius (Dyfrig), 2

Earconwald, St, 90
Edward of Norwich, Duke of York, 34, 76, 82, 90, 182

Index

Edward, Prince of Wales ("the Black Prince"), 19, 42, 55, 104, 181, 185
Edward I of England, King, 35
Edward II of England, King, 45
Edward III of England, King, 1-2, 23, 30, 45, 50, 57, 61, 64, 66, 69, 71, 86, 88, 98, 104, 118, 142, 151
Edward IV of England, King, 153
Edward VII of the United Kingdom, King, 8
Elizabeth I of England, Queen, 7, 51, 161
Elmham, Thomas, 53, 57, 84
Eltham Palace, 45, 90, 169
Epiphany Rising, 13, 30, 57
Eric of Norway, King, 16
Erpingham, Sir Thomas, 81
Eu, 71, 111, 172
Évreux, 103, 112-3, 175

Falaise, 102-3, 175
Fanhope, Lord, 144, 183
Fastolf, Sir John, 63, 153, 183
Fécamp, 71
Fitzalan, Joan, 16
Fitzalan, Thomas, 5th Earl of Arundel, 34, 37, 182
Fitzalan, William, 22
Flint Castle, 13
Fluellen (fictional character), 6-7
Fresnay-sur-Sarthe, 112
Frileuse, 63
Fricourt, 75

Gamaches, Guillaume de, 143
Gamaches, Philippe de, 143
Gaucourt, Raoul de, 65-6
Geoffrey of Monmouth, 5-6

Giles, Master, 65
Gill, Will, 159
Gisors, 111, 116, 177
Glyndyfrdwy, 25
Goodrich, 9
  Castle, 32
"Grace Dieu", 96
Graville, Priory of, 63-4, 173
"Great Work", 46-7
Greenwich, 63
Grey, John, Earl of Tankerville, 138, 184
Grey, Thomas, 62, 186
Grosmont, 32
Grosmont, Henry of, 15
Grouchy, Jean de, 67
Gwladus Ddu, 16
Gwladys, wife of William ap Thomas, 56

Hall, Edward, 153
Hardy, Robert, 157
Harfleur, ix, 54, 62-71, 76, 79-80, 90, 92-97, 105-6, 111, 144, 146, 149, 170-1, 173
Harlech Castle, ix, 31, 34-7, 65, 168
Harlescott, 24, 27
Harold Godwinson, King of England, 3, 97
Hastings, Battle of, 4, 100
Henry II of England, King, 116
Henry IV of England, King, 1, 3, 7, 9, 11-14, 16-20, 23-5, 27-30, 38-44
Henry V of England
  as King, vii-ix, 3, 5-6, 15, 42-151
  as Prince of Wales, ix, 12-41
  birth, viii, 1-3, 16, 32

193

childhood, 5-12, 15-16
death, vii, ix, 146-50
Legacy, 2-3, 7, 151-9
Henry VI of England, King, 62, 119, 135, 145, 151, 153, 155, 160, 185
Henry VII of England, King, 7, 49, 150, 161
Henry VIII of England, King, 2, 22, 52, 154
Henty, G A, 159
Holland, John, Earl of Huntingdon, 96, 103, 106, 112, 138, 184
"Holy Ghost" (ship), 96
Honfleur, 99, 102, 111
Howard, Robert, 123
Humphrey, Duke of Gloucester (brother of Henry V), 8, 60, 78, 82, 93, 95, 103, 106, 146, 151-2, 183
Humphrey, Earl of Buckingham (died 1399), 12, 185
Hus, Jan, 47, 92

Ireland, viii, 11-13, 55, 62
Isabeau of Bavaria, queen consort of France, 108, 115, 132, 146, 185
Isabelle of Valois, queen consort of England, later Duchess of Orleans, 12, 16, 60, 85
Isleworth, 47
Ivry, 111

James I of Scotland, King, 43, 48, 53, 96, 136-7, 158, 186
Jandun, Jean de, 125
Jean de Bourbon, 59
Jean d'Alençon, 59
Joan of Arc, 110

Joan of Arc's Tower (Rouen), 110, 113, 176
Joan(na) of Navarre, queen consort of England, 11, 50, 59, 85, 102, 148
John of Gaunt, 1-3, 10, 12, 14-15, 27, 45, 50-52, 160, 185
John, Duke of Bedford (brother of Henry V), 8, 60, 89, 92, 117, 160, 185
John, Duke of Brittany, 11, 59, 101, 118
John the Fearless, Duke of Burgundy, 59, 74, 84, 93-5, 104-8, 115-6, 119, 122, 133, 186

Kenilworth Castle, ix, 26-30, 50-53, 60, 105, 153, 168
Kidwelly, 45, 56
King's Daughter (cannon), 36
Kings Langley, 42

La Roche-Guyon, 111
Lambeth Palace, 91, 93, 169
Lancaster (duchy), 3, 14, 33, 42, 44, 51, 56-57,
Le Havre, 62-4, 66-7, 170-1, 173
Le Mans, 112
Leicester, 8, 10, 46, 51, 137, 165-6
    Castle 14-15, 44, 137, 165
    Earl of, 51
Linet, Robert de, 108
Llywelyn the Great, 16
Loire (river), 133, 142
Lollards, 15, 45-7, 93
London Museum, 8
Louis VII of France, King, 147
Louis IX of France (Saint Louis), King, 117, 120-2, 127, 130, 134, 141

Index

Louis, Duke of Orléans, 58-9
Louis of Guyenne ("the Dauphin Louis"), 58, 85, 96, 101, 113, 118, 185
Louviers, 104-5, 175
Louvre, 50, 128, 130, 132-4, 146, 178
Lune (river), 51
Lydgate, John, 61, 65, 90, 152

Maisoncelle, 76, 171
Mametz, 75
Mantes, 114, 117, 176
Marie of Brittany, 11
Matilda, queen consort of England, 71, 98, 100
Matilda, Empress, 109
Maud, Countess of Cambridge, 62
Maud, Countess of Salisbury, 9, 38
Meaux, 143-7, 178
Melbourne, Peter, 14
Meulan-en-Yvelines, 114-5
Melun, 122-4, 131, 176
Messager (cannon), 36, 65
Milford Haven, 12
Monchy-Lagache, 74
Monmouth, viii, 3-7 164-5
    Castle, 2-3, 164
Monnow (river), 2, 4
Monstrelet, Enguerrand de, 76, 132, 152
Mont Cabert, 64
Mont Lecomte, 64, 66
Mont-Saint-Michel, 111
Montagu, Lady Margaret, 8-9
Montagu, Thomas, 8, 38, 97, 184
Montereau, 116, 122, 178
Montivilliers, 71, 111
Morgan, Philip, 112
Morley, Lord, 95, 184

Mortimer, Edmund, 23, 30, 36
Mortimer, Edmund, Earl of March, 11, 28, 30, 43, 61, 184
Mortimer, Roger, Baron Mortimer (died 1282), 16
Mortimer, Roger, Earl of March, 2, 11

Naudin, Pierre, 159
Neelpot (cannon), 36
Nesle, 73-4, 173
Nesle, Guy de, 145
Notre Dame de la Rose, Abbey of (Rouen), 105

Ogmore, 32
Oldcastle, Sir John, 45-6, 63, 186
Olivier, Laurence, 54
Order of the Garter, 12, 24, 46, 93
Orne (river), 98
Oxford, viii, 11, 41, 45, 166, 181
Owain Glyndŵr, 5, 7, 17-18, 29-36

Page, John, 152
Pale of Calais, 69, 86
Pargeter, Edith, 21
Paris, 50, 58, 68-9, 104-9, 113-8, 122-35, 140, 142, 145-8, 159, 170, 178-9, 185
Percy, Elizabeth, 23, 28, 186
Percy, Henry, 1st Earl of Northumberland (1341-1408), 13, 17, 33, 186
Percy, Henry ("Harry Hotspur"; 1364-1403), 17-18, 23-8, 30, 33, 44, 81, 158, 187
Percy, Henry, 2nd Earl of Northumberland (1393-1455), 43-4, 187

Percy, Thomas, 1st Earl of
    Worcester, 17, 23, 25-6
Péronne, 72-3, 75, 173
Peterborough, 8, 48
Philip the Good, Duke of
    Burgundy, 116-8, 122-3, 125,
    140, 146-7, 186
Philippa, Duchess of York, 134
Philippa of Hainault, queen consort
    of England, 2, 93
Philippa, queen consort of Norway
    (sister of Henry V), 8, 185
Philip(pe) II of France, King, 73,
    111, 114, 130, 149
Philippe IV of France, King, 57
Poitiers, Battle of, 56
Pont de l'Arche, 105
Pontefract, 13, 137
Pontoise, 104, 114-8, 135, 179
Portchester Castle, 61, 180
Portsmouth, 63, 97
Powys, John Cowper, 37
Prince of Wales (title), ix, 8, 12, 14,
    18, 39, 43, 45, 55, 137

Queen's College, Oxford, 11, 166

Raglan Castle, 56
Rhys Ddu, 34
Rhys Gethin, 32
Richard, Duke of York, 62
Richard, Earl of Cambridge, 61-2,
    160, 186
Richard, Earl of Cornwall, 49, 57-8
Richard I of England, King, 1, 100,
    109, 111-2, 114, 151
Richard II of England, King, viii,
    1-2, 9-14, 16, 18-19, 23, 28, 37,
    39-40, 42-4, 48, 63, 77, 87, 151
Robert III of Scotland, King, 17, 43

Robessart, Sir Lewis, 149, 184
Rouen, 48, 67, 71, 99, 103-11, 113,
    117, 135, 148, 152, 176-7
    Cathedral, 112, 177

Saint-Étienne, abbey of (Caen), 98
Saint-Faro, abbey of (Meaux),
    143-5
Saint-Remy, Jean Le Fèvre de, 152
Saint-Trinité, abbey of (Caen), 98
Salic Law, 57-9
Scrope, Lord, 62, 186
Seine (river), 63, 65, 67, 92, 94, 99,
    105-6, 114, 122, 128, 130-3
Sens. 119. 121-3, 179
Severn (river), 2, 19, 21, 24
Shakespeare, William, vii, 6-7, 29,
    54-5, 58-9, 63, 65, 80-1, 85,
    154-8, 160
Sheen Abbey, 48
Sheen Palace, 48-9, 52
Shrewsbury, 19-24, 26, 28-9, 31,
    166-7
    Abbey, 21-22
    Battle of, viii-ix, 24-8, 30-1, 51,
        55, 78, 80, 90, 158, 166-7
    Castle, 20
Shropshire Regimental Museum, 20
Sigismund, Holy Roman Emperor,
    92-5
Somme (river), 71-4
Southampton, 55-7, 94, 96, 186
    "Southampton Plot", 61-2,
        156, 186
Spithead, 63
Stafford, Anne, 61
Stafford, Edmund, 8th Earl of
    Stafford, 25
Stewart, Murdoch, 43
Strecche, John, 105, 153

Index

Swynford, Katherine, 10
Sycharth, 25
Syon Abbey, 46-8, 169
Syon House, 48, 169

Talbot, John, Earl of Shrewsbury, 32, 36, 95, 187,
Taurin(us), St, 113
Thomas of Lancaster, Duke of Clarence, 8, 31-2, 38, 40, 60, 64-5, 68, 97, 99, 103-5, 117, 122, 134, 138, 140, 184
Thomas of Woodstock, 1, 12, 87
Titchfield Abbey, 57, 61, 180
Tito Livio dei Frulovisi, 151
Touraine (duchy), 61
Tournebu, Richard de, 97
Tranter, Nigel, 159
Trecastle, 56
Tretower, 56
Trim Castle, 12, 62
"Trinity Royal", 63
Troy House, 8
Troyes, ix, 102, 118-22, 177
Troyes, Treaty of, 118, 120-1, 124, 135, 139, 153
Tudor, Owen, 158, 160
Turberville, Sir Payn, 31
Twenge, John, 35, 137

Usk, 33

Valmont, Battle of, 68
Vincennes, ix, 50, 147, 180

Visconti, Lucia, Countess of Kent, 136

Walton, William, 156
Waring, Johanna, 8
Warminster, 56
Waterton, John, 14
Welsh Bicknor, 2, 8, 165
Westminster, 46, 93
    Abbey, ix, 12, 42, 47, 90, 136, 149, 170
    Palace, 49-51, 93
Whitchurch, 26, 167
Whitelock, John, 43
Whittington, Richard ("Dick"), 47
William ap Thomas ("Blue Knight of Gwent"), 56, 184
William Longsword, 109
William, Duke of Bavaria, 93-4
William I of England, King ("William the Conqueror"), 71, 97-98, 100, 102, 116
William II of England, King, 116
Windsor Castle, 50, 139, 144, 160, 185
Wingfield's Tower, 20
Wolvesey Castle, 60-1, 180
Worcester, William, 153
Wycliffe, John, 45
Wye (river), 2, 8-9
Wyngaerde, Anton van den, 48

Yonge, Charlotte M, 158